# LEFT COAST LIBATIONS

Left Coast Libations
P. O. Box 16064
Oakland, CA 94610
www.leftcoastlibations.com

Produced by Scott Bodarky and Michael Lazar
Book Design by Lisa Hoffman

Additional photography by:
Heather Hawksford (p 66, ten01, Portland)
Weston Henderson/50 Grit Studios (p 86, Vessel, Seattle)
Steve Li (p 118, West, Vancouver)
Trujillo Paumier (p 12, The Varnish, Los Angeles)
David Lanthan Reamer (p 127, Clyde Common, Portland)
Jennifer Yin/Eater SF (p 26, Smuggler's Cove, San Francisco)

ISBN 978-0-9826315-0-8

10 9 8 7 6 5 4 3 2 1

Printed in China
First printing, 2010

Some recipes in this book specify brands of spirits or other ingredients when the bartenders thought it made
a difference in the resulting cocktail. Left Coast Libations received no consideration for specifying brands,
and has paid for all of the ingredients used to test the recipes.

# TABLE OF CONTENTS

# ACKNOWLEDGEMENTS

First and foremost, I must acknowledge the fundamental contributions my big brother Charles F. Munat made to Left Coast Libations. It was Charles who first had the idea of a book that not only provided outstanding original cocktail recipes, but also promoted the creators of those cocktails while highlighting the Left Coast. It was he who coined the term Left Coast Libations, he who was my collaborator on the original Left Coast Libations booklet, and he who sprung for the cost of having them printed. Suffice to say, without Charles, there would be no Left Coast Libations, and you would currently have nothing in your hands, and you would be staring at your lap like some sort of sad sack.

I say all this about Charles in the most sincere yet non-legally binding way, of course.

Unfortunately, in the epilogue to the original Left Coast Libations booklet, Charles asked the reader to please kill him if he ever considered creating another cocktail book. When word began to spread that another Left Coast Libations was in the works, we found that there were many, many people all too willing to take him up on this request. So we decided for his own safety it would be best for him to sit this one out.

Next, I'd like to thank Paul Clarke, Robert Hess, Marleigh Riggins, Maria Hunt, Gwydion Stone, Anita and Cameron Crotty, Blair Reynolds, and Erik Ellestad. All of these fine folks were contributors to the original LCL, but were sadly not included in the version before you, as we elected to go exclusively with professional bartenders (Blair and Erik, by the way, have since become professional bartenders in a transparent and desperate attempt to gain inclusion in this book. If you see either of them, do not tell them where I am or how to get ahold of me).

Essentially, we used the names, reputations, and creations of these people to pave the way for our own success, then tossed them aside like so much trash. And they've all handled this abuse with admirable grace and good nature...more or less. Plus, now one day I can tell my grandchildren that Robert Hess, the "Cocktail Messiah," once called me a "bastard."

OK, actually it was twice.

And further thanks to Mr. Ellestad and Ms. Riggins for acting as my (unpaid) consultants in hatching a list of Bay Area and Los Angeles bartenders. If you are a bartender in either of those areas and feel slighted not to be included, you really need to take it up with those two. Thanks again Erik and Marleigh!

Since we have been operating on a shoestring budget (frayed, mismatched shoestrings at that), we have relied heavily on the generosity and patience of the artists who have put their work into this book. They all have worked in kind or at significant friends and family discount rates, and have held our shivering novice hands through the various processes. And for that, we owe them a debt of gratitude. So thank you, unfathomable amounts, to the brilliant Jenn Farrington, who churned out the cocktail photographs in this book (plus about 1000 more) in two wild days at Flora in Oakland. Beyond even her work as a photographer, Jenn's enthusiasm for this project and excitement to be involved was both flattering and inspiring.

Thank you to Tom Schnitz at Flora for graciously allowing us to use his beautiful, beautiful bar for our photo sessions. And thank you to Erik Adkins and Lane Ford for babysitting us while at Flora. Perhaps I'm engaging in wild speculation here, but I'd imagine you both have better things to do on your days off than sit at one of your places of work and watch us place cocktails on tables and take pictures of them, while I whine that the Wi-Fi keeps going out. And keeping in that same vein, thank you to Daniel Hyatt for permitting us use of his lovely bar Alembic—twice in fact—for subsequent re-shoots (prizes available for those who can guess which photos are from Alembic!).

Thanks to Greg Boehm of Mud Puddle Books for his wisdom, advice, and support. Greg went out of his way again and again to do everything in his power to help get this book into your hands. If you see this man, kiss him...unless you sense he really doesn't want you to.

Thank you to Jenny Adams, writer extraordinaire and all around barrel of laughs, for all her work in getting the book on the lips of readers, writers, and drinkers everywhere.

Thank you to Ed "The Legend" Ledger of Ledger's Liquors in Berkeley for helping us to source the liquors needed to test, make, and photograph the drinks. If you are a fan of cocktails and fine spirits and you have yet to go to Ledger's Liquors, then you probably have no concept of what happiness and fulfillment are. Sorry to be the bearer of such news. And Ed, if you're out there, thanks for all the Willetts.

Thanks also are due to Mr. Scott Bodarky, the uncredited partner of Left Coast Libations. Scott's experience and expertise in book publishing, along with his many months of hard work, are why this book is actually printed words on paper, as opposed to me standing on a street corner shouting out drink recipes and bartender biographies (but if you don't like to read I will totally meet you somewhere and do that). Despite all this, Scott toils in anonymity. So let's give him his moment, shall we? Thanks Scott! Really!

And of course, words will never adequately express my gratitude to all 51 of the contributors to this book. Thank you for your recipes, your support and encouragement, for putting up with dozens of follow-up emails asking for clarifications on this and that, and for your friendship...not to mention all the hugs and kisses. This book is about you, and this book is for you. Thank you. You are beautiful.

**Ted Munat**
*From a solitary barstool somewhere on the Left Coast*

This book is dedicated to
Charles Elliot "Chuck" Munat
25 April 1934 - 6 June 2009

Peace be with you, Papa.

# FOREWORD

In the 13th century something very important happened. No, the cocktail wasn't invented. That happened at least twelve hundred years earlier, when Jesus turned water to wine, then steeped it in herbs and mixed one part of it with two parts bourbon and a dash of bitters.

In the 13th century, Rumi—by all accounts a learned, distinguished gentleman and scholar, a teacher and mentor to many fine young students—rode a donkey into town and met Shams—widely known as a mad man and heretic street preacher. Witnesses to this celestial event claim that Shams posed a theological question to Rumi so profound, so overwhelming in its wisdom, so consciousness-altering in its poignancy, that Rumi would later proclaim that what he once thought was God appeared to him that day as a man. Overcome with this chance encounter with the Beloved, Rumi fainted and fell from his donkey to the ground.

The same thing happened to me once. Except instead of a donkey, it was a barstool.

Dear reader, this book is for you. We made it just for you. Never mind what I wrote in the acknowledgements about it being for the bartenders. I was just sucking up. And the bartenders by now, having ensured that their asses have been properly kissed, have long since skipped ahead to find their own profile pages and bask in their own awesomeness. So we're free to speak openly now.

We offer this book to you not only as a useful text in and of itself, but as a portal into a community, a community brimming with creativity and exploding in its scope.

Left Coast Libations (LCL) will not be the first source to preach about the creative talents of bartenders, or of the esteemed role in a community a bartender can and should (and will again!) hold. Nor shall we be the first ones to hail the renewal in appreciation for the fine work that they do.

LCL may, however, be the first to take these claims so deeply to heart. While newspaper and magazine articles tout the accomplishments of bartenders, the bartenders themselves are often misrepresented, their drink recipes butchered. The shelves of our bookstores continue to be filled with cocktail recipe books offering little to no credit to the creators of the drinks within their pages. It is with these continued slights in mind that we offer this book, of and about bartenders, but for us all.

Make no mistake about it, this is also every bit a cocktail recipe book. Some of the finest bartenders in the world have graced us with the creations of which they are most proud. Each recipe has been painstakingly created and tested. The most minute details of the recipes have been analyzed, discussed, and then clarified. Every effort has been made to ensure that each recipe in this book is clear enough to be re-created as intended by anyone with the tools, ingredients, and gumption to try it...unless you screw it up. Don't screw it up!

But at the end of the day, what is a cocktail book but a static list of words, a snapshot of a fluid process that changes and grows by the moment? Buddhists are always happy to tell us that the universe destroys itself and then is re-created every moment, in a continuous cycle for eternity. And so is the case with cocktails. The creation and re-creation is always happening. It is happening somewhere right now. Somewhere, something new has just been created. Did you feel it? You missed it, didn't you? Try to pay closer attention. Whoops! It just happened again. Did you catch it that time? Good job!

In the end, even the most intelligently designed cocktail book is scarcely a substitute for actual participation in this process. The process is alive and evolving, and LCL plans to evolve with it. We are hereby extending an invitation for you to participate as well.

So read the recipes, make or buy the ingredients required to make them, and enjoy. But please, do go seek out the women and men featured in this book, have a drink, learn from them, and tip them. Big.

**Ted Munat**
*Somewhere in an aeroplane in the sky over the Left Coast*

# INTRODUCTION

by Paul Clarke

"The greatest accomplishment of a bartender," wrote Harry Johnson, a pioneering practitioner of the craft, "lies in his ability to exactly suit his customer." What Johnson didn't cite in his 1882 *Bartender's Manual* (and why would he, really? The notion of a blogger with frequent-flier miles and a taste for creative cocktails was still more than a century off) but which has become common knowledge among the 51 bartenders featured in this book is, "Always give recipes and guidance to Ted Munat. God knows he needs the help."

Okay, that's not entirely true. Ted is a talented mixologist in his own right, and besides, Harry Johnson would likely have ignored a time-traveling Ted had he ever spent any time propping up Johnson's bar—though whether that's because Johnson would have been too preoccupied with promoting his own legacy behind the stick to have paid attention to a 21st century drink writer, or because as a New York bartender he likely exercised a willful ignorance of the goings-on along the Pacific coast (oh, how some things never change) is a matter for boozy debate.

But whatever Johnson's reasons for ignoring the bearded drinker smiling politely and, likely, blearily at him from above the rim of a rapidly disappearing whiskey cocktail, there are several things that would have been certain, had these two ever met: first, as an amateur enthusiast of mixology, Munat would have peppered Johnson with questions until eventually, whether out of helpfulness or exhaustion, Johnson would have shared some secret for what was going into his mixing glass (and Ted, should you ever get the chance with that time-travel machine: find out what's in Johnson's orchard syrup, would you, please?); second, as an ardent supporter of talented bartenders, Ted would take what Johnson revealed to him and share it with others in the profession and with other thirsty enthusiasts, sowing the seeds (as it were) of mixological wisdom in the fertile terrain of West Coast bars; and finally, probably around the time his recipes began circulating on the Internet—not that they had the Internet back then, but play along, I'm making this up as I go—Johnson would

have come to the realization that somewhere amid the flurry of flattery and the muddle of mumbled jokes, Munat had managed to wheedle Johnson out of not only his secrets, but of a half-dozen drinks as well.

Of course, Harry Johnson didn't experience the pleasure of having Ted Munat sit at his bar, an empty glass in front of him and a beseeching expression on his face. The same can't be said for any of the West Coast bartenders featured in this book.

*Left Coast Libations* covers not only some of the West Coast's best bartenders and the drinks they create; it helps reveal their mixological philosophies and their dedication to the craft—not to mention their boundless patience at answering Ted's questions. From the nouveau speakeasies of Los Angeles to the culinary watering holes of San Francisco to the fine restaurant bars of Vancouver, and from the cutting-edge creativity of Portland bartenders to the classically oriented stylings of Seattle's drink slingers, Munat has managed to coax recipes and techniques from some of the finest bartenders plying the craft today.

Their mixological styles may differ, but each demonstrates excellence in taste and hospitality. In short, each of these bartenders embodies Johnson's guiding principle: whether they see bibulous beauty in a simple mixture of gin and vermouth, or if their path to the perfect drink takes them through the farmer's market and the molecular laboratory, their greatest accomplishment lies in their abilities to suit each of their customers. While a wander through the recipes in these pages won't give the reader quite the same pleasure as bending an elbow while seated at one of these bars, it will provide some insight into the talents of today's creative bartenders.

So break out the mixing glass and open up the liquor cabinet; it's time to embark on a liquid exploration of the West Coast. ~Cheers~

# ON READING THE RECIPES
# AND MAKING THE COCKTAILS

᎔ There are 102 cocktail recipes in this book and 41 of them call for some sort of homemade ingredient, from the very simple (Honey Syrup) to the most sublime (Smoked Cider Air). These ingredients have been marked with an asterisk (*) in the cocktail recipes that follow. The recipes for making these ingredients have been collected and alphabetized in the appendix. There you will also find notes on various bartending techniques that will be of particular interest to the neophyte (and possibly the expert as well, if only to harrumph and contradict).

᎔ Cocktail ingredients are listed either by quantity (from most to least) or, for cocktails where it matters, in the order in which they are needed (which Ted believes is an abomination against God). Garnishes are always listed last.

᎔ Whenever a recipe reads: "all the ingredients" this excludes any garnish.

᎔ All fruit juices and herbs are to be fresh unless otherwise noted. Store citrus at room temperature if it is to be squeezed. This maximizes the amount of juice you will get out of each piece of fruit.

᎔ Simple syrup is 1:1 (sugar to water ratio) unless otherwise noted. A recipe is included in the appendix.

᎔ Zests, strips, twists, spirals, discs, and shavings ("hay") are all forms of citrus peel to be used as a garnish. It is ideal to peel citrus as needed for each cocktail, since fresher is always better. I will add that many bartenders consider it anathema to include any of the white pith on their citrus peels but it can be hard to prepare them so every time. (For an excellent guide to preparing citrus peel garnishes, see Dale DeGroff's *The Craft of the Cocktail*. Dale also does a great job showing how to flame an orange peel disc.)

᎔ A barspoon (one of those long-handled things, often with a twisted stem) is the equivalent of about one teaspoon.

᎔ A dash is, for better or worse, a highly variable quantity, dependent on both the physical bottle in which the ingredient is stored, as well as the "oomph" of the hand using it. There is no substitute for experience (or taste) when making a cocktail that calls for dashing.

- A mixing glass is the same as a pint beer glass, one with thick walls and base. The glass must also be tempered to minimize the chance of breaking.

- A shaker is always a two-part Boston-style shaker, never a cobbler shaker. If you are shaking with a tin and a mixing glass (as opposed to two tins), always point the glass end away from anyone who may be standing nearby in case of breakage.

- A muddler is a tool used to press or, in some cases, smash, dry ingredients, such as peels, fruits, and herbs in a mixing glass to release flavors. Muddlers can be made from a variety of materials, but the best ones are milled from hardwood or a solid plastic (Delrin) rod.

- Double-straining refers to the technique of using a Hawthorne or julep strainer over the mixing glass/tin and then pouring the contents through a small fine strainer into the cocktail glass. Among other things, this catches pulp from fresh juices and results in a clearer cocktail.

- See the appendix on homemade ingredients for a discussion on frothing egg whites.

WARNING: Raw eggs may be a health hazard for people with compromised immune systems, the elderly, or women who are pregnant. Use caution when serving cocktails containing whole eggs or egg whites to people who may be at risk.

- See the appendix on homemade ingredients for a discussion on ice.

Now: Enjoy!

- **Michael Lazar**

    *Not as hung over as he expected to be*

# ALPHABETICAL LIST OF COCKTAILS

# ALPHABETICAL LIST OF BARTENDERS

LOS ANGELES is a city both idolized for its glamour and derided for supposedly being the earth's premier bastion of all things shallow and superficial. In the basin of this conflict of stereotypes, a small but dedicated, talented, and growing number of bartenders are resurrecting an authentic and elegant aspect of Los Angeles cultural history. No, they are not espousing the spiritual and cultural beliefs of the Chumash tribes who settled in this valley thousands of years ago. Nor are they kneeling before shrines in honor of Junipero Serra, the Franciscan friar who established a mission here in 1771. (But someone really ought to name a drink after him, I mean come on!)

No, the folks you are about to read about, along with several others, are well into the process of re-discovering the golden era of cocktails in Los Angeles. Think about it for a moment and it all makes sense. After all, where do you think they made all those old films that portrayed cocktail swilling as such a debonair and sophisticated act? That was a golden era, an era when films taught us important lessons, lessons such as: "Damn you're sexy and charming when you have a martini in your hand!"

Many of these bartenders hail from the cocktail Mecca of New York City and bring this inspiration west, where they have incorporated it into the culture and cuisine of Southern California. And over time they have increasingly communed with their fellow Left Coasters to the north to increase the cocktail gene pool and build our glorious Left Coast community. The result is a truly unique and eclectic collection...a delightful mixture...a cocktail, one might even say.

# LOS ANGELES

The Varnish

# ERIC ALPERIN

I'm an LA ignoramus. In some circles they call this a LAgnoramus. What circles, you ask? Secret circles. Very small, very secret circles.

So when approaching LA, I asked for recommendations from the small circles of bartenders in cities more familiar to me, such as San Francisco, Portland, and Seattle. Eric Alperin was on everyone's short list. When I asked him about being in the book, he responded with such enthusiasm and positivity, I figured he must be some up-and-coming bartender, newer to the industry, eager to get further involved. It wasn't until doing some research (yes, research was involved in the making of this book, contrary to appearances) that I realized the man has done everything and knows everyone. Apparently my ignoramusness (yes that is a word, don't bother to look it up...it is) extends far beyond LA. Further apparent is the fact that Eric's enthusiasm comes not from being new, but from having an unbelievable level of sustained passion for what he does.

Before getting into the bartending stuff, it should be mentioned that Eric acts, and in 2004 starred in a short film titled "Basic Emotions," in which he assumed the role of "Hot Guy." Internationally renowned film critic Jay Kuehner proclaimed his performance "metaphysical yet ornithological." Jay's weird.

Eric started bartending in New York City, getting his indoctrination by fire making mass quantities of cocktails at The Screening Room (a lounge/restaurant/film venue) before getting more into craft cocktails at Lupa. At the latter, Eric says he made cocktails with an Italian accent, which makes me imagine him saying "Hey-a you-a, I'm-a gonna make-a you a nice-a Sazerac! Oh! What'sa matta for you, eh?"

In all seriousness, at Lupa he was exposed to amari and grappas. Excited by this, Eric exposed himself to them. Grappas are a tricky cocktail ingredient to work with, but when a bartender learns how to make effective use of them, they hold the keys to other dimensions of cocktail complexity and elegance. Yeah. I said that.

Eric next worked alongside Sasha Petraske at Milk and Honey and also Little Branch. He went through the reportedly brutal but esteemed Beverage Alcohol Resource (BAR) program, where he passed despite his Spiccoli-like insistence on having pizzas delivered to his desk in the middle of class. Then he busted the hell on out of there and joined us on the Left Coast.

He landed at Osteria Mozza, where he ran the show, created the cocktail list, paired cocktails with food, and lorded over his staff with a mighty iron fist. It was then on to the Doheny, and then a reuniting with Sasha, this time as co-owners of The Varnish in downtown LA. I must go to this place, and so must you. Meet me there. Wire me a plane ticket first though.

And one further note on Eric's move from NYC to LA...In your FACE East Coast! We got your boy! Oh, it burns, don't it? Don't it burn?

Pardon the trash talking please. It's in my blood. I am, after all, from the East Coast yo.

Smuggler's Notch

## Smuggler's Notch

*à la Sazerac...*

1 brown sugar cube

3 dashes orange bitters

2 oz. dark rum

Absinthe or Herbsaint

Orange twist, for garnish

*Notes:*

*The sugar should be dissolved before straining this cocktail. Brown (raw) sugar cubes take more time to dissolve than refined white sugar. Chilling the cocktail (i.e. putting ice in the mixing glass) means it will take even longer.*

꙰ Muddle the sugar cube and bitters in a mixing glass.

꙰ Add the dark rum and ice.

꙰ Rinse a whiskey glass with the absinthe or Herbsaint.

꙰ Stir and strain the cocktail into the prepared whiskey glass.

꙰ Garnish with an orange twist, being sure to spray the top of the cocktail with the oils from the peel.

## Kingsbury

½ oz. Campari

½ oz. Dolin dry vermouth

½ oz. Licor 43

½ oz. lime juice

Prosecco

Long, thin slice of cucumber, for garnish

*Notes:*

*The prosecco should be brut, not extra dry.*

꙰ Combine all the ingredients, except the prosecco, over ice.

꙰ Mix using a "light toss" (a gentle, five-second shake).

꙰ Strain into a champagne flute.

꙰ Top with prosecco.

꙰ Garnish with the cucumber.

# CHRIS OJEDA

Like many of the bartenders in this book, Chris Ojeda is a lifer, having started in the food service industry when just a pup, working his way up the ranks from busser to bartender. Like many of the bartenders in this book, Chris didn't realize in the beginning he would be a lifer, having instead thought his career would be determined by his attendance at something called 'college.' Snort. What's that?

Chris worked for years at what he describes as "corporate establishments," creating cocktail and training programs and fostering a lineage of bartenders whom he mentored. During this period he also created (along with fellow LCL'er Marcos Tello) Drinks First, Questions Later, a mobile cocktail catering company specializing in handcrafted cocktails, fresh squeezed juices, and homemade syrups... OK, they actually were selling shots of hooch out of an ice cream truck at playgrounds. Don't you judge them!

Chris traveled to New York, studied cocktails with Gary Regan and other "dignitaries" (term used loosely and with a touch of irony, of course), and made a pilgrimage to Milk and Honey, where a young bartender with a gleam in his eye and a song in his heart, Eric Alperin, was plying his trade. Eric and Chris's paths would eventually cross again, this time on the Left Coast, at Osteria Mozza. Eric established a cocktail program emphasizing amaro apertivi at Osteria, and Chris then carried that torch, continuing to emphasize fresh, seasonal ingredients and Italian apertivi.

Chris is also helping to revive the speakeasy lifestyle in Los Angeles through The Radio Room at The Edison. The Radio Room is a place to find many of Southern California's best bartenders making exquisite cocktails from the golden era with the utmost attention to proper technique. The ambiance has been likened to that of the old Cocoanut Grove, but with a healthier respect for fire codes and a much cooler website. Chris most recently has rejoined Eric Alperin at The Varnish. Chris apparently plans on horking up every cool bartender job in LA. Wish him luck.

Finally, Chris co-operates the cocktail consulting company For Medicinal Purposes along with fellow LCL'ers Damian Windsor and Marcos Tello. Chris describes himself as "the third leg" of this endeavor, which, to say the least, conjures up some pretty graphic images. And we'll leave you with that image. Get yourself to LA, if you've ever wanted to see the third leg in action.

# Fior di Sicily

¾ oz. Averna amaro

¾ oz. Carpano Antica Formula vermouth

¾ oz. Aperol

¾ oz. St. Germain elderflower liqueur

Orange peel, for garnish

- Stir all the ingredients with ice for 30 seconds (wet ice) or 50 seconds (large ice).
- Strain with a julep strainer into a chilled cocktail glass.
- Flame the orange peel over the cocktail then drop in the peel.

*Notes:*

*I think by "wet ice" Chris means the kind you'd buy in a bag at a supermarket and then let sit about in a picnic cooler. By "large ice" Chris means chunks of ice you'd hew from a large commercial ice block with an ice pick or possibly KOLD-DRAFT cubes.*

# Fragola e Aceto

1 fresh strawberry, hulled

½ oz. Simple Syrup*

2 oz. Plymouth gin

½ oz. lime juice

3–4 turns of fresh cracked black pepper

3 drops of aged balsamic vinegar

Basil Foam*

Fresh basil, for garnish

- Muddle the strawberry and the simple syrup in the bottom of a mixing glass.
- Add the gin, lime, and black pepper.
- Shake over ice.
- Double-strain into a chilled cocktail glass.
- Add the balsamic with an eyedropper.
- Top with the basil foam.
- Lay one very teeny tiny basil leaf on top of the foam.
- Take a handful of basil and clap it together over the top of the drink, so that the essence of the basil is left behind, and discard.

Fragola e Aceto

# JOSEPH BROOKE

Joseph is another escapee from the East Coast who settled comfortably into the Left Coast. East Coast, mend your fences! In Joseph's case, he claims to have taken the plunge not for some esteemed career opportunity behind the bar, but rather for his two vices: "acting and a girl." One might be tempted to imagine a surprise twist in this tale, in which the girl turns out to be his young daughter, who Joseph struggles to raise all on his own after her mother dies tragically, while he wonders if he'll ever find true love again. But, in reality, I think it was probably someone about his age who he had the severe hots for and so he did the lovesick boy thing and headed westward.

The point is, Joseph has turned out be a working actor, but is a genuine star behind the bar. He started bartending in New York, first at Starfoods, then at Amy Sacco's Bette. Then came the move to LA. And let it be known that Joseph's move was not some impetuous act. Prior to packing his bags, he put in some inquiries and determined that they did in fact have bars in Los Angeles, and that they paid people money to serve alcohol in them. This bit of knowledge in hand, he made the journey across our great nation, undertaking an odyssey so bizarre, circuitous, surreal, and involving circus freaks that it will one day be documented in an epic novel that offers a fresh perspective on the American experience.

Either that or he hopped a plane, took a nap, and when he woke up his girlfriend was there to give him a ride from the airport. Whatever. They're both great stories.

Joseph went to work making quality cocktails at Bar Marmont, before moving to The Edison in 2007. These days, he works at Copa d'Oro in Santa Monica, two blocks from the beach, under the tutelage of "Los Angeles Cocktail Deity" Vincenzo Marianella.

Let's all take a moment to wish we were Joseph, shall we?

OK, back to the story. At Copa, they buy produce from down the road at the Santa Monica Farmer's Market and turn it into things such as...well, whatever you want really. The cocktail menu at Copa, in addition to some deliciously boozy house cocktails, also provides a list of base spirits, fresh herbs, fruits, vegetables, juices, and seasonally available produce. Patrons are encouraged to choose items from any or all of the lists and let their bartender create something for them. In Joseph's case, if he makes a drink this way and it turns out bad, he just blames the patron for "choosing stupid stuff."

No, he doesn't. Did I mention he's an actor? Joseph admits that to use this book to promote his acting career would be both shameless and embarrassing, but he did pay me $500. So go to josephbrooke.net and make fun of him. Then cast him in your new film, the one based on that epic novel that offers a fresh perspective on the American experience.

The Lively

## The Lively

1 large fresh strawberry

2 oz. gin

¾ oz. Agave-Ginger Syrup*

¾ oz. lemon juice

Splash of Simple Syrup*

↪ Slice one-quarter of the strawberry off and set aside for a garnish.

↪ Muddle the remaining ¾ strawberry with all the other ingredients.

↪ Shake over ice.

↪ Strain over fresh ice into a sour glass or a small Collins glass.

↪ Garnish with the reserved quarter strawberry.

*Notes:*

*Joseph says a new western dry gin works best in this cocktail, such as Martin Miller's Westbourne Strength. Tanqueray 10 would be another option.*

*I would recommend double-straining this cocktail.*

## The Brass Flower

1 oz. gin

1 oz. grapefruit juice

¾ oz. St. Germain elderflower liqueur

2 dashes Fee Brothers grapefruit bitters

Brut champagne

Strip of grapefruit peel, for garnish

↪ Gently toss (a five-second shake) all the ingredients, except the champagne, over ice.

↪ Strain into a chilled champagne flute.

↪ Top with the champagne.

↪ Twist a strip of grapefruit peel to express the oils over the drink, discarding the peel.

↪ "Drink and laugh."

*Notes:*

*Joseph says Plymouth or a London dry gin works best in this cocktail.*

*The grapefruit juice used for this cocktail should not be too sweet.*

## Historic Core Cocktail

1½ oz. Rittenhouse 100-proof rye

½ oz. Laird's Bonded apple brandy

½ oz. green Chartreuse

½ oz. Carpano Antica Formula vermouth

1 generous dash Angostura bitters

Lemon peel, for garnish

↬ Stir all ingredients with ice.

↬ Strain into a cocktail glass.

↬ Garnish with the lemon peel.

*Notes:*

*John says you may also try using cask-strength Thomas H. Handy Sazerac rye in place of the Rittenhouse.*

## Seven Sins

1 oz. Sazerac 6-year-old rye

1 oz. Laird's Bonded apple brandy

¾ oz. lemon juice

¾ oz. Grenadine*

Cinnamon stick, for garnish

↬ Shake all the ingredients over ice.

↬ Strain into a cocktail glass.

↬ Grate some of the cinnamon stick over the top.

Seven Sins

# JOHN COLTHARP

We talk a lot in this book about people who fled the East Coast to the Left Coast, and I talk a little smack from time to time about it. In John Coltharp, we have a different and perplexing form of fugitive. John was born and raised in the Pacific Northwest, specifically in Chimacum, Washington, a small peninsula town just south of Port Townsend. Then he moved to Los Angeles. I guess I'm OK with that...as long as he doesn't root for the Lakers...or the USC football team.

I like to envision John wandering the forests of the Olympic Peninsula as a lad, collecting huckleberries and salmonberries and Oregon grape and miner's lettuce, hand chipping chunks of glacier ice with the same knife his great granddaddy used to build a shelter when the family first settled in the area, bringing all of it back home to mix with the apple brandy he made in a pot in the shed. Yep. That's some genuine bullshit right there, but it's my very own bullshit.

John reports feeling more comfortable among the bears of the Northwest woods than the denizens of LA's urban jungle, despite having been in Los Angeles for seven years. He tends bar at Seven Grand, your standard "Swank Irish" lounge with black walnut bar, hundreds of whiskeys, and...mounted Jackalope heads? Guess that must be an LA thing.

This just in: Seven Grand has a pool table. Repeat: has a pool table. It joins Touché in Portland (James Pierce) as the only bars mentioned in this book with reported incidents of pool tableism.

John would also like to throw his name into the pool of bartenders to list Seattle's Murray Stenson as an influence. He also lists Sammy Ross of New York City and fellow LA LCL'ers Eric Alperin and Marcos Tello as important figures in his development as a bartender. That's three corners of the contiguous United States covered. If anyone has a Miami bartender they can pair John up with, he would really appreciate the symmetry. After all, to a bartender, balance is everything.

John classifies his approach to drinks as "less is more." Keep it simple. Many of the top bartenders feel this way. And they're right. Three or four carefully chosen ingredients in the right proportions will always make the most perfect, timeless cocktails. But when telling people about this book, you can be damn sure I'll be prattling on about amino-acid-infused-demiglace-prickly-pear-and-hibiscus-jam. Or some lunatic ingredient like that. It gets people's attention. John doesn't seem to need the attention. He's one of those fringe types that take pleasure in the simple craft of bartending and the extension of hospitality to his guests...must be another LA thing.

# DAMIAN WINDSOR

I was just reading Damian Windsor's industry bio and I passed out. It was too much information. My insistence on holding my breath until it was all over didn't help. So please, before you read this, remember: breathe.

Damian's career in the service industry began in Australia as a room service waiter. I imagine one day he was bored waiting for the elevator and started combining the OJ, wine, and scotch on his cart, and thought to himself, "I wish I had some flippin' Cherry Heering on this cart! How am I s'posed to mix up a Blood and Sand? And would it be too much to ask for some KOLD-DRAFT ice?" Frustrated by having to operate under such conditions, Damian quickly became a manager and bartender and thus began his whirlwind tour of planet Earth.

Damian first came to the U.S. in 2001 to open Theo Bar in some place called New York City, where he also consulted for Carnaval cocktail bar. His first advice to the latter was that they spell their name correctly, but they refused. An outraged Damian fled back to Australia, discouraged.

I am making up the silly parts of this bio, by the way. The true-sounding stuff is real. This will be your only disclaimer.

Months later, Damian boarded a plane back to New York City with the intent of exacting revenge upon Carnaval's management by making them all over-diluted Manhattans without bitters. Unfortunately, his plane was hijacked to Toronto where he was forced to root for the Blue Jays, and he worked at Bruyea Brothers. He eventually made his way back to New York, but only in a surreal dream brought on by ingesting kielbasa before bedtime. In the dream, he worked for a sunburnt cow named Chris Johnson.

Excuse me. I got that incorrect. He worked at a restaurant and bar called The Sunburnt Cow, which was owned by Chris Johnson. And it wasn't a dream. It was real.

At this point, Damian finally pulled his head out of his ass and moved to the Left Coast, where he... Nope, got that wrong too. Next he moved to Miami. Miami? There he worked for Shoji Sushi and Shingo Inoue and many other Japanese words as well. Then, finally, he moved to the Left Coast in 2005 and went to work for the Hungry Cat, which he found to be a much better-tempered animal than the Sunburnt Cow.

In addition to The Hungry Cat, he worked a slew of spots around LA before moving to Seven Grand three days after their opening. Once again suffering from a severe case of ants in the pants, Damian proceeded to undertake bartending engagements at Gordon Ramsay at The London, Copa d'Oro, Bar Lubitsch, and The Edison.

And now, in honor of this book, Damian has taken his bartending skills and helped open a brand new frikkin' frakkin' bar in Los Angeles. It's called The Roger Room. It is brand new, but already is known in LA as the premier place to get rogered. Damian, in his own words, is, "ecstatic" at this development.

Did you remember to breathe?

Sbagliato Grosso

## Montresor and Fortunato

1½ oz. Emilio Lustau amontillado sherry

¾ oz. Grand Marnier

½ oz. Carpano Antica Formula vermouth

Lemon peel, for garnish

Orange peel, for garnish

3 Queen olives, for garnish (see note, below)

*Notes:*

*Queen refers to the size of the olive—any commonly available large green Spanish olive should do. These should be pitted and not stuffed.*

⌒ Stir all the ingredients with ice.

⌒ Strain into a cocktail glass.

⌒ Twist the lemon peel and then the orange peel over the cocktail to express the oils and discard.

⌒ Garnish with the olives on a pick.

## Sbagliato Grosso

1 strawberry, hulled

1½ oz. Hennessy VS cognac

1 oz. Campari

1 oz. sweet vermouth

½ oz. Ricard pastis

2 dashes Angostura bitters

Lemon peel, for garnish

Orange peel, for garnish

*Notes:*

*Damian says you can use Noilly Prat or Martini Rossi red vermouth for this cocktail.*

*The instructions say "press gently" on the strawberry but don't be afraid to press it firmly enough so that it releases enough flavor into the cocktail. Just don't mash it.*

⌒ Place the strawberry in a large rocks glass and press on it gently to crush.

⌒ Add ice and the rest of the ingredients.

⌒ Stir to chill.

⌒ Twist the lemon peel and orange peel over the drink to express the oils.

⌒ Garnish with the peels.

## Whiskey Barrel Punch

*Serves 12*

The thin-cut peels of three lemons

2¼ oz. superfine sugar

8 oz. lemon juice

4½ oz. Monin pomegranate syrup

½ bottle (375 ml) Woodford Reserve bourbon

4 dashes of Angostura bitters

Brut champagne (approximately ¼ of a bottle)

- Muddle the lemon peels with the sugar until the oils are well expressed and the sugar is moistened.
- Add the lemon juice and stir until the sugar has dissolved.
- Remove the lemon peels from the mixture.
- Add the pomegranate syrup, bourbon, and bitters.
- Add ice and stir again.
- Strain into a punch bowl over a large block of ice and top with the champagne.

*Notes:*

*Marcos says you may use homemade pomegranate syrup (grenadine) instead of the Monin, but if you do, you may want to increase the amount of sugar you add.*

*Any high rye content bourbon, such as Bulleit, may be substituted for the Woodford Reserve.*

## Alexandria Hotel Cocktail

1 oz. cachaça

1 oz. Campari

½ oz. Mathilde peach liqueur

2 dashes orange bitters

Orange peel disc, for garnish

- Stir all the ingredients with ice.
- Strain into a cocktail glass.
- Flame the orange peel disc over the surface of the drink and discard the peel.

*Notes:*

*Marcos recommends using a bitters mixture of half Fee Brothers and half Regan's No. 6.*

Alexandria Hotel Cocktail

# MARCOS TELLO

Marcos Tello is resident mixologist at The Edison in Los Angeles...and so, so much more.

For starters, he is co-creator, along with Chris Ojeda, of the liquid catering company Drinks First, Questions Later and also For Medicinal Purposes, a cocktail consulting operation that provides training and menus to restaurants and bars. Through his work with the latter (a collaboration with Damian Windsor and that Ojeda guy again) he has created and implemented new cocktail programs at Seven Grand, The Doheny, Malo, and The Edison. Any of those places sound familiar? Good! Your reading comprehension is stellar!

Marcos is also on a mission to create and sustain a cocktail culture in Los Angeles, and carries out this mission in such a multitude of ways as to make it impossible to describe or quantify. He launched The Sporting Life, a collective of bartenders and cocktailians determined to create a cocktail community in Southern California through meetings, cocktail events, competitions, and brute force if necessary (hasn't been yet, thank God.) The Sporting Life has also helped build momentum toward revitalizing the Southern California chapter of the United States Bartenders' Guild (USBG), and Marcos has his hands all up in that as well.

I managed to get myself on Marcos's mailing list, and over the past months I have received notice of cocktail competitions, meetings of the newly formed USBG chapter, Cinco de Mayo celebrations at Malo, opportunities to join Gary Regan's Worldwide Bartender Database, cocktail events featuring some visiting bartender named Jackie Patterson, a workshop on ice featuring some guy named Jon Santer, a collaborative project between LA rock bands and bartenders, and Marcos' 30th birthday...to list just a few.

Incidentally, as a birthday present to himself, Marcos ran the freaking LA Marathon. I think he's a cyborg.

There's plenty more to report on Marcos's community building efforts, but I can't forget to mention that he's a bartender. That hasn't been said once yet. Go back and check. It's true. He's actually nothing short of a great bartender. Marcos has started working with a whole mess o' LCL'ers at The Varnish, and remains at his main digs, The Edison, a place steeped in the history of cocktails and of Los Angeles, both areas of passion for Marcos. (Did I mention he's a budding historian of Los Angeles cocktail culture and lists cocktail historian David Wondrich as a mentor? I didn't? Dammit! I can't pull everything together with this guy. There's just too much.)

Marcos just needs a whole book all to himself. Anyone want to pay me to write that?

SAN FRANCISCO is the 800-pound gorilla of the Left Coast cocktail world. But it's a kindly gorilla, a gorilla not unlike the one who saved that kid who fell into the gorilla exhibit at the zoo that one time. (This is actually quite a literal analogy; I once fell in San Francisco, and many of the city's finest cocktail minds picked me up, dusted me off, and served me another drink.)

The depth and breadth of exceptional bars and bartenders in the Bay Area is breathtaking. You can spend a month there and still not get to every bar you should. You can put more Bay Area bartenders in your bartender book than from any other area and still leave out dozens of deserving ones. The Bay Area is actually kind of annoying like that.

But it is an area bursting with creativity and spirited exuberance. A night spent with the keepers of the Bay Area cocktail culture is something akin to attending a party planned by the Marquis de Sade and being held simultaneously in the Weimar Republic and Caligula's Rome. May their blessed cocktail empire never fall!

# SAN FRANCISCO

Smuggler's Cove

# DANIEL HYATT

Daniel is an understated sort of fellow who seems unconcerned with the art of self-promotion, but perhaps he's aware that there are already forces in motion around him that seek to propel his legend. That is to say, if one spends time with bartenders and cocktail aficionados, one hears many a tale of the genius Daniel Hyatt of Alembic in San Francisco. Stories are circulated about such topics as his victory in a major cocktail competition with a drink he'd never tried before but intuitively knew would work—a drink whose proportions he nailed on the first try. Bartenders who travel to San Francisco return to their native cities speaking of Hyatt, the wizard, working wonders on Haight Street.

Bartenders also love Alembic, where Daniel is head bartender and part owner. And there is a definite lesson to be learned from this: in an age of high and higher concept bars that often run from pretentious to downright gaudy, the bar that engenders the most awe and warm regard is a simple, homey, welcoming little spot, that also happens to make cocktails that will blow your fragile little mind. Zane Harris, after guest bartending there, said that if he were to open his own bar, he would want it to be like Alembic.

Daniel described Alembic to me as a punk rock bar. Fair enough. When I finally had the chance to witness it myself I found the staff listening to Japanther, a Brooklyn-based punk duo noted for songs such as "Buried Alive" and "Dump The Body In Rikki Lake" (which would also be a great name for a cocktail, by the way). Enjoying the fractious strains of such artists while sipping a perfectly crafted cocktail featuring celery juice or maple syrup gastrique was not an experience I anticipated this life would afford me. Yet there it was.

While the feel of the bar and the service itself smacks of the friendly neighborhood tavern, this is balanced by Daniel's avant-garde explorations in the cocktail realm. His brilliance in this area seems to be the result of his refusal to be bound by any pre-existing conceptualization of what a cocktail is or should be. He will create a drink in any shape or form, bending the dimensions of the drink in acquiescence to the ingredients, rather than attempting to force the ingredients into a shape familiar to us.

I think in some circles that's known as creativity. In fact, I reckon some folks may even be inclined to dub it genius.

## Southern Exposure

1½ oz. Old Potrero Junipero gin

¾ oz. Celery Juice*

½ oz. lime juice

½ oz. Simple Syrup*

5–6 mint leaves

Mint leaf, for garnish

- Shake all the ingredients over ice.
- Double-strain into a chilled cocktail glass.
- Garnish with the mint leaf.

Still Life with Apples, After Cézanne

## Still Life with Apples, After Cézanne

2 oz. Evan Williams Single Barrel bourbon

½ oz. Maple Syrup Gastrique*

Smoked Cider Air*

Sprig of fresh thyme, for garnish

- Stir the bourbon and gastrique over cracked ice.
- Strain into a thin cordial glass or a champagne flute.
- Spoon the froth from the smoked cider air over the top of the cocktail.
- Garnish with the sprig of fresh thyme.

*Notes:*

*You might also try serving this in a traditional absinthe glass, which is similar to what Daniel uses at Alembic (see photo).*

# BROOKE ARTHUR

Everybody, everybody, everybody loves Brooke Arthur. And Brooke Arthur, as best as I can tell, loves them right back. Brooke once referred to herself as a girl from Chico who lucked her way into the cocktail industry. Here's a map of what luck looks like:

She left Chico and worked restaurants in South Lake Tahoe at age 19, before moving on to Santa Rosa and learning all about wines at Portofino. She then moved to San Francisco without a place to stay and got herself a job as a server at the Redwood Room in the Clift Hotel, where Erik Carlson tended bar and Duggan McDonnell was soon to assume bar manager duties. She opened half a dozen restaurants around San Francisco, training the service staffs, before Erik presented her with the opportunity to train as a bartender at Umami, where he was now bar manager. She took the opportunity, and soon she was also tending bar at Range where, according to Brooke, "I worked under Carlos Yturria who taught me about seasonal ingredients, Dominic Venegas who improved my spirit knowledge and taught me how to make a tough all booze cocktail, Camber Lay who taught me about infusions, Thomas Waugh, and Mike La Freniere—all still my mentors and the people that I owe all the credit to." Within a year she was promoted to bar manager at Range. Accolades and brushes with fame ensued.

Note the humility her tale is lined with, paying homage to all those who taught her and helped her along the way. It is left to us to review and discern that Brooke has experience in a litany of environments, roles, and venues; and she has extensive knowledge in wine, spirits, infusions, seasonal ingredients, and bar craft.

She has studied under some of the great minds and spirits of the cocktail world, and she now has become one herself. She may not know it yet. She may also not realize that she is one of the rare people whose mere presence imbues those around her with a sense of well-being and comfort. And this is why everybody loves Brooke Arthur. But it's possible she doesn't know why yet. If you see her, will you let her know?

Poppies in October

## Poppies in October

1½ oz. Sazerac 6-year-old rye

¾ oz. Aperol

½ oz. Marie Brizard Apry apricot brandy

3 dashes Qi black tea liqueur

2 dashes Regan's orange bitters

Lemon peel, for garnish

☙ Stir all the ingredients for 40 seconds.

☙ Strain into a chilled rocks glass (no ice).

☙ Flame a lemon peel into the glass and drop in for garnish.

*Notes:*

*It can be difficult to find Marie Brizard products in some markets. The Rothman & Winter Orchard Apricot can be used as a substitute.*

## Evergreen

4 kumquats

3 large sage leaves

½ oz. lemon juice

1½ oz. Plymouth gin

1 oz. St. Germain elderflower liqueur

1 large sage leaf, for garnish

☙ Muddle the sage and kumquats with the lemon juice.

☙ Add the remaining ingredients, shake hard 20 times.

☙ Double-strain into a chilled cocktail glass.

☙ Place the remaining sage leaf in the flat of your hand and then smack it with the other hand over the top of the cocktail.

☙ Place it on top for garnish.

## The Matador

1¼ oz. Highland Park 12-year-old scotch

1¼ oz. Dry Sack 15-year-old oloroso sherry

¾ oz. Aperol

Orange tie, for garnish (see note, below)

- ⮑ Stir all the ingredients over ice.
- ⮑ Strain into a cocktail glass.
- ⮑ Garnish with the orange tie.

*Notes:*

*Dry Sack is made from a particular blend of dry and sweet sherries and I would not substitute another oloroso for it.*

*A tie is a long thin strip of peel with an overhand knot loosely tied in it.*

Pear Sonata

## Pear Sonata

1½ oz. Plymouth gin

1 oz. St. Germain elderflower liqueur

½ oz. lemon juice

½ oz. dry vermouth

¼ oz. pear eau de vie

Pear Foam*

Dash of cinnamon, for garnish

Pear slice, for garnish

- ⮑ Shake ingredients (except for foam) over ice.
- ⮑ Double-strain into an ice-filled Collins glass.
- ⮑ Top up with pear foam.
- ⮑ Garnish with the cinnamon and the pear slice.

*Notes:*

*Joel prefers Vya vermouth for this cocktail but says Cinzano works as well.*

*Don't use an overly large Collins glass for this cocktail. An 8-ounce glass should be plenty big.*

# JOEL BAKER

Joel is a fine young gentleman who was kind enough to be part of the original, underground, no-budget *Left Coast Libations* booklet the Munat Bros. printed up in 2008. However, he neglected to provide us with proper biographical information, despite our repeated threats to write a fictional and quite silly biography for him should he fail to do so. As a result, I wrote a silly bio for him. So silly, in fact, that I imagined it would stand as a lesson in the future to all bartenders that they should indeed send detailed biographical information, lest they go the way of poor, ridiculed Joel.

But instead, everyone ended up liking the bio, most of all Joel. And bartenders all figured it would be way more fun to have me make stuff up than accurately represent their lives and accomplishments. Instead of a cautionary tale, Joel became a hero, a shining knight. And when this book came about, Joel predictably suggested we just run the same bio as before. So without further ado, The Joel Baker Story, folks!

"Joel Baker has assumed the responsibility of bar manager at Bourbon & Branch after, gosh, quite a bit of time as bartender there. Always recognizable by the stylish hat perched upon his finely-shaped head, he looks even more stylish now with the large, flashing 'BOSS' sign pinned to his lapel.

"Prior to working at Bourbon & Branch, Joel probably worked in other bars that were really freaking cool, but not quite as cool as Bourbon & Branch. Otherwise, he'd still be there and not at Bourbon & Branch. Unless, of course, he got fired. That's always a possibility.

"Didn't he win some awards or something? Yeah, we're sure he did. Probably lots of 'em."

Incidentally, Joel continues to this day as manager of Bourbon & Branch, always seems to be traveling somewhere to compete in something, and makes mighty wonderful drinks. And he really does have a finely shaped head. I wouldn't kid about something like that.

## 606

1½ oz. genever gin

½ oz. sweet vermouth

½ oz. Fernet Branca

Orange twist, for garnish

➴ Stir all the ingredients gently with ice.

➴ Strain into a chilled cocktail glass.

➴ Garnish with the orange twist.

## Old Bill

1 oz. oloroso sherry

½ oz. maraschino liqueur

½ oz. aged rum

3 dashes orange bitters

➴ Stir all the ingredients gently with ice.

➴ Strain into a small wine glass.

*Notes:*

*Oloroso sherries can vary quite a bit in terms of dryness. I used Lustau East India sherry, which is pretty sweet, and it dominated the cocktail. You may want to try a drier one.*

*Neyah says he prefers Ron Zacapa rum if it is available.*

Old Bill

# NEYAH WHITE

In a true gesture of love and admiration, Neyah White provided the author with some unique information about himself specifically for the readers of *Left Coast Libations*. It is therefore with a healthy measure of excitement that we present Neyah, uncut...

**A List of Favorites:**

Word: Righteous

Drink: Dealer's Choice—let the bartender do what he/she does best.

Mobile: iPhone

Desktop: PC

Super Hero: Wolverine...of course.

Super Villain: Skeletor

Author: Yates, Richard

Heat Source: White Oak (I'm American, I like oak in everything)

This, folks, is the sort of insider glimpse into the secret lives of bartenders only *Left Coast Libations* can provide. Tell your friends.

Neyah, like quite a few contributors to this book (not to mention its author), is an East Coast kid who found his way to the Left Coast. And gosh darn it if he didn't like it. Neyah's been tending bar for more than 15 years, both East and West, and counts himself as fortunate to have fallen into the booming San Francisco cocktail scene. In addition to having a good old time making drinks behind the bar, Neyah's interests extend to making his own bitters, tinctures, and liqueurs. Nopa, the sprawling and bustling (and fantastic) restaurant and bar where Neyah is bar manager, is noted for its array of all these items. And yeah, that's mostly Neyah's fault. That's why he's got that little smirk on his face. He knows he's a bad, bad man. Neyah is also fully on board with working with local farms to get the best seasonally available products for his drinks, and allowing this natural availability to dictate the direction of the cocktail menu. What a concept.

Neyah is even interested in distilling. Did you know that? I didn't know that! He's visited distilleries all over the world, and completed the Whisky Academy program at Bruichladdich, Scotland, under the legendary Jim McEwan. That experience woke Neyah up to the fact that the surplus of former wine barrels in California could be put to use for aging his own whiskey and rum. Neyah says these spirits are still "sleeping," but plans to release them when they wake. Wake them gently, please Neyah. Spirits are fragile little critters.

# H. JOSEPH EHRMANN

H., another East Coast refugee, has been working in the restaurant industry since 1986, with some detours. At one point, he went to something called "college," earned something called an MBA, went someplace called Europe, and did something called corporate consulting. What will they think of next?

Tired of immersing himself in such senseless abstractions, H. returned to his original love: booze. It's always heartwarming when people do that. And he returned with a vengeance, transforming one of the oldest saloons in San Francisco into Elixir, which then became the first bar to be certified as a Green business by the City of San Francisco. So one of the oldest became the first. Talk about senseless abstractions!

As best as I can gather, Elixir's certified green-ity comes from H.'s emphasis on local products, of both the farm-fresh and the distilled variety, and using environmentally conscious products such as the non-paper labeled, soy ink printed Square One Organic Vodka, for whom he is National Brand Ambassador. It should also be noted that H. rarely turns on the air conditioning in his Hummer H3 while he's commuting to and from work.

I bet H. doesn't really drive a Hummer.

In 2006, H. founded Cocktail Ambassadors, a consultancy for bar and restaurant operators as well as the product and service companies that supply them. He has designed custom cocktails and beverage programs for hotels, bars, and restaurants, as well as for product companies and exclusive private clubs.

H. is a graduate of the prestigious Beverage Alcohol Resource (BAR) training program, vice president of the San Francisco chapter of the United States Bartenders' Guild (USBG), and co-founder of the The Barbary Coast Conservancy of the American Cocktail (BCCAC)—the organization responsible for bringing us San Francisco Cocktail Week (SFCW). H. Joseph Ehrmann (HJE) will put his collection of initials and acronyms up against anyone in the nation! His begins with HJE and continues with an MBA, and just gets wilder from there. So think twice before you step to him.

Celery Cup No. 1

## Celery Cup No. 1

1-inch round of freshly peeled English cucumber

2 2-inch celery stalks (closer to the heart for sweetness)

A palmful of cilantro leaves (about 1/4 cup)

1 oz. lemon juice

1½ oz. Square One Cucumber organic vodka

¾ oz. agave nectar

½ oz. Pimm's #1

⌁ In a mixing glass, muddle the cucumber, one of the celery stalks, cilantro, and lemon juice into a pulp.

⌁ Add the Pimm's, agave nectar, and vodka.

⌁ Cover with ice and shake hard for 10 seconds.

⌁ Strain over fresh ice into a small (8 oz.) Collins glass.

⌁ Garnish with the second celery stalk.

Notes:

*H says:* "This play on a popular Pimm's Cup variation is very versatile, cool, and refreshing. Try this one and then play with it to come up with No. 2, No. 3, and so on. Variations: add 1/4 of a kiwi to the blend or try a touch of salt or a seasoning blend like lemon pepper on the rim of the glass."

*After making many of these, I'd modify the instructions a bit: cut the cucumber round into a number of smaller pieces, put into the glass and muddle hard by itself. Add the celery (include a few leaves) and muddle hard again. Finally add the cilantro and muddle until things are starting to get very wet. Then add the lemon juice and muddle some more. You really want to extract as much flavor from the "green matter" as possible.*

## La Tuna Te Toca

1½ oz. Del Maguey Crema de Mezcal

1 oz. Prickly Pear Juice*

1 oz. lime juice

½ oz. agave nectar

½ oz. maraschino liqueur

Long lime twist, for garnish

⌁ Shake all ingredients over ice for 10 seconds.

⌁ Strain into a cocktail glass

⌁ Garnish with the long lime twist.

Notes:

*H says:* "When available try one or both of these additions to this cocktail: Sal de Gusano and Chapulines." *(See the appendix for descriptions of these ingredients.)*

# LANE FORD

There is a growing perception in certain communities today that bartenders, when truly operating at the peak of their profession, actually ascend to such a level as to be considered artists. One often hears talk of the art of the cocktail, the art of bartending, or cocktails as a culinary art form. To this I must first report that I have personally attempted to gain acceptance from certain art cooperatives by describing my cocktail pursuits as an art form; and I can safely say the perception of cocktails as art has not infiltrated the arts community itself.

But were those artists, or any other doubters, to witness Lane Ford make drinks, or to speak with him for a bit about cocktails, they would likely come a long way towards being convinced. When Lane speaks of fellow bartenders he admires—such as Thad Vogler or Eric Johnson—he speaks in terms of creative epiphanies and re-conceptualization of what a cocktail is. The phrasing and vocabulary, if taken out of context, could easily be mistaken for Sonny Rollins effusing about John Coltrane, O'Casey praising Joyce, or Chuck Jones speaking on Tex Avery. It's inspiring.

Lane's also an extremely nice person—humble, not a self-promoter, and quite an amazing bartender.

A former New Orleanian, Lane now quietly blows heads up around the Bay Area with his cocktail skills. His former posts include Beretta, Oakland's Flora, and Heaven's Dog. Last time I saw him at Heaven's Dog, he made me a Mint Julep that had me contemplating thusness while metathinking suchness. Ha! Bet you never had a cocktail that did that to you. He made it with some sort of divine antique rye that I was too drunk and stupid to bother to remember. That wasn't Lane's fault though.

More recently, Lane spearheaded the bar program at Starbelly, brought to you by the same folks who brought us the mighty Beretta. At Starbelly, Lane worked exclusively with wine and beer, but still mixed drinks, such as the Madeira Cobbler or a Shandy of beer and lemonade. Starbelly continues to build upon the trend toward partnerships between bars and farmers, actually displaying full profiles of the farms they work with on their web site. Lane now continues his relationship with the Beretta management team at the newly opened Delarossa, a restaurant and bar in San Francisco's Marina district in much the same vein as Beretta. Yes, they are once again allowing Lane to mix the hard stuff. Look out world.

I wish Lane would come out and play more often. But I know when and where to find him behind a bar. That's one of the things I love about bartenders. For at least a few hours per week, they're sitting ducks.

## The No. 4

*"a dandy of a recipe to ease the nerves and go down like velvet"*

2 oz. reposado tequila

¾ oz. lemon juice

¾ oz. Grapefruit Syrup*

½ oz. egg white

2 dashes absinthe

Grapefruit peel, for garnish

⌁ Dry shake all the ingredients.

⌁ Add ice and shake again.

⌁ Double-strain into a coupe.

⌁ Garnish with a grapefruit peel.

## Arrack Sour

*"a woody elixir brought to you by the mixing of Indonesian culture with Dutch traders. A mind-altering concoction that should be put down first and then no more for the rest of the night"*

1½ oz. Batavia Arrack

¾ oz. lemon juice

½ oz. maraschino liqueur

½ oz. Simple Syrup*

½ oz. egg white

2 dashes Peychaud's bitters

Lemon twist, for garnish

⌁ Dry shake all the ingredients.

⌁ Add ice and shake again.

⌁ Double-strain into a coupe.

⌁ Garnish with the lemon twist.

Arrack Sour

# CHRISTINE D'ABROSCA

Some elements of Christine's background are pretty familiar amongst the LCL crowd. Like many of us, she hails from the East: Rhode Island, in fact. And like many, she dabbled in that arcane pursuit known as college. And like many, she started bartending out of need to eat while studying. And like many, something in the aromas of her cocktails awakened her senses, and she realized that to bartend is divine and that the Left Coast is where it's at.

Christine credits Steve Olson, and his company "aka wine geek," with starting her on the path to bartending glory. Steve emphasized to her the importance of working in conjunction with the kitchen and utilizing fresh and seasonal ingredients. Christine, the child of a family who loved to cook, and the fiancée of a sous chef, found this approach resonated with her, and to this day she still has a passion for the Farmers' Market and cocktail-food pairings.

When Christine came to Los Angeles in 2007, she had the opportunity to work at Seven Grand. She was the only woman behind the bar there. But hey, she can handle it. She cites the experience at Seven Grand as being one of intense growth and learning, and credits her coworkers there with the tip on an opening at Malo, where Christine went on to become Beverage Director.

Malo is a Mexican restaurant and bar on Sunset Boulevard where the bar—and their selection of tequilas—gets top billing. The tequila list stands at over 150 and counting, all of which are 100% agave, and it also includes dozens of mezcals. Christine has helped create a beautiful cocktail menu of drinks mostly based on tequila, incorporating that bounty of Farmers' Market produce, while at the same time nodding to a classic style of cocktail composition. It all reminds me of what Mexican feminist and author Gloria Anzaldua described as the coming together of opposite qualities within—hieros gamos. When those opposite qualities come together, an epiphany occurs: they are not actually opposites, but complementary pieces to the same puzzle. Which means we can have the best of all worlds without fear of conflict. Which means, in this context, yummy cocktails. Oh goodie!

So, you're not going to believe this, but next Christine moved to San Francisco! The rich get richer. And upon arrival there she went to work at Smuggler's Cove. Glance about the San Francisco section of this book and you will note that Matty Eggleston, Dominic Venegas, and Jackie Patterson are all also working "The Smove," as absolutely no one calls it. I will assume at this point you have put this book down and are racing to "The Smove" to see Christine and others, and I will therefore take the opportunity to write whatever I want since no one is listening: In he be the to of that was at it! Give get going when have the fall feel better high time!

For those of you too lazy to have left, you have been rewarded for your lethargy with a rare glimpse into the author's inner mind. Now get to Smuggler's Cove already.

## St. Astor

1¾ oz. Ron Matusalem 17 year Grand Reserva rum

½ oz. Tahitian Vanilla–Infused St. Elizabeth Allspice Dram*

½ oz. Grand Marnier

½ oz. lime juice

Candied Orange Wheel*, for garnish

Mint sprig, for garnish

- Shake all the ingredients over ice.
- Strain over fresh ice into a rocks glass.
- Garnish with the candied orange wheel and mint sprig.

## Easy Like Sunday Morning...

2 oz. Gran Centenario Rosangel tequila

¾ oz. pineapple juice

¾ oz. lemon juice

½ oz. Aperol

2 dashes Angostura bitters

1 dash Fee Brothers orange bitters

1 small egg white

Jarritos Jamaica soda (see note)

Long thin strip of orange peel, for garnish

- Dry shake all the ingredients except the soda for 15 seconds.
- Add ice and shake again.
- Strain into a Collins glass over fresh ice.
- Top with a splash of the Jarritos Jamaica soda.
- Garnish with the orange peel wrapped around a straw to make a spiral.

*Notes:*

*The pineapple juice should be canned 100% unsweetened juice, not from concentrate. This is one of the few times we don't call for fresh juice.*

*Jamaica (pronounced "ha-mai-ka") refers to the dried flower petals of Hibiscus sabdariffa or a dark red infusion made from them. It is a very popular beverage in Mexico, where it is sweetened and served as an alternative to regular black iced tea. Jarritos is a brand of bottled Mexican soda that offers a Jamaica flavor. This is most easily found in grocery stores specializing in Latin American foods.*

St. Astor

## In 2 Deep

1½ oz. Partida reposado tequila

¾ oz. Domaine de Canton ginger liqueur

½ oz. Punt e Mes

1 barspoon Fernet Branca

2 dashes orange bitters

Wide orange twist, for garnish

⌒ Stir all the ingredients with ice.

⌒ Strain into a small cocktail glass.

⌒ Garnish with the orange twist.

## Blueberry Nights

1¾ oz. Plymouth gin

¾ oz. Dimmi liqueur

½ oz. lemon juice

4–5 fresh blueberries

1 large sprig fresh lavender

Wide lemon twist, for garnish

⌒ Shake all the ingredients over ice.

⌒ Strain into a cocktail glass.

⌒ Garnish with the lemon twist.

*Notes:*

*Dimmi used to be called Veloce di Milano.*

*I would recommend lightly muddling the blueberries and the lavender before shaking this drink. I think Kevin probably counts on the berries and lavender getting sufficiently bruised during shaking to add flavor and color because he has access to very hard ice cubes.*

*You can use dried lavender as a substitute for the fresh sprig, but you will need to reduce the quantity, because the dried buds are much stronger than the fresh; about ⅛ tsp. of the dried flowers should be enough.*

Blueberry Nights

# KEVIN DIEDRICH

Kevin Diedrich is one of the best bartenders in the world. But he's been living and working on the East Coast lately. Screw this guy. He's out of the book!

Although, he really is a great bartender, and we all really love him a lot. And he promises he's coming back... Nope. Traitor. Out of the book!

OK, he's back in the book. For a few reasons. One is my faith that vanaprastha, the Taoist sage's return to the forest, will occur (the Left Coast being the forest and Kevin being the sage). Another reason is that we, the Left Coast, claim him and will not relinquish rights to him. The third reason is that, well, we can't live without him, and therefore our psychological well-being hinges upon believing he will be back soon. Kevin? You out there?

So here goes. Kevin is from the East Coast, and got his start in bartending about six years ago in the Washington, D.C./Arlington, Virginia area. He started in clubs, then got a job at the Ritz Carlton D.C. One day, Kevin went to work at the Ritz Carlton D.C., and it magically transformed into the Ritz Carlton San Francisco. And that's how he came to move to the Left Coast.

After some time at the SF Ritz, Kevin landed a bartending gig at the then-brand-new Bourbon & Branch. For Kevin and all the boys working there at the time, this was a period of elevation in the craft, as they each inspired one another. Kevin then moved to Clock Bar in the Westin St. Francis Hotel, intrigued by the opportunity to work with LCL'er Marco Dionysos, while still helping out at The Branch when called upon. In the meantime, he acted as general manager for Cask, the lovely and immaculately stocked liquor store owned by the Bourbon & Branch team, and was an instructor at San Francisco's Beverage Academy.

It was around that time—early 2009—when Kevin had the chance to reinvigorate the cocktail program at Bourbon Steak, Four Seasons Hotel, in Washington, D.C. He took it, but he promises he's coming back. While there, Kevin is bringing what he learned in SF back to D.C. and also introducing products not readily available in that area.

Wait. He's what? He's stealing our ideas and our booze and shipping them back East? That's it Kevin! You are officially out of the book!

P.S. Love ya! See ya soon?

P.P.S. Kevin wanted me to mention that he slays dragons.

San Francisco

42

# YANNI KEHAGIARAS

True story: As the deadline approached to get recipes for this book, none had yet come from Yanni. Making the situation even more dire, my only method for contacting Yanni was an email address associated with Bourbon & Branch, which was no longer valid in light of Yanni's recent move to Nopa. I sent an email out to the other Bay Area contributors to LCL, and enlisted them in finding Yanni and getting drink recipes out of him. I took this bit of strategy from Gunnery Sergeant Hartman in Stanley Kubrick's *Full Metal Jacket*, who, in an effort to motivate Private Pyle, inflicts hard labor upon the rest of the company each time Private Pyle "fucks up."

Yanni, AKA Private Pyle, did not kill me and then blow his own brains out all over the bathroom wall, because that's Hollywood bullshit. Instead, he sent me some drink recipes, stating that the SF Bartender S.W.A.T. team had stormed his bedroom that morning.

I know Yanni. I've sat at his bar (and also stood next to it once). He's a great, great bartender and a beautiful man. But he's never told me about his past, and I never had the heart (or stomach) to ask. And I didn't want to call in the SF S.W.A.T. team again...that whole thing about it being "a sin to kill a mockingbird" rang in my mind.

So instead, in honor of Yanni, I solicited random statements from people on Facebook to complete his bio. It's hard to explain, but I just knew Yanni would want it this way.

*"I first met Yanni when he was an extremely devoted bar manager at The Cheesecake Factory. That sunovabitch owes me ten bucks! What about the time he got blacked out drunk then took off all his clothes and went bridge jumping? I heard Yanni K. was married to Jocelyn Wildenstein, AKA the Cat Lady, in 1999. Apparently Yanni kept falling asleep in bed while smoking, causing Jocelyn's millions of dollars in plastic surgery to melt away in places. This resulted in a very private, but very nasty, divorce."*

(Special thanks to LCL'ers Jackie Patterson, Joel Baker, and Chris Churilla, along with this weird guy I know named Ben, for contributing to this piece.)

Yanni really is a fabulous bartender and a special guy. He worked at Bourbon & Branch as a bartender and sometimes manager, and now reigns alongside Neyah White at Nopa. What more do you really need to know? He's Yanni for God's sake!

Incidentally, Yanni claims he'll go ton-for-ton mining coal with any man or woman in this book! The gauntlet has been thrown down!

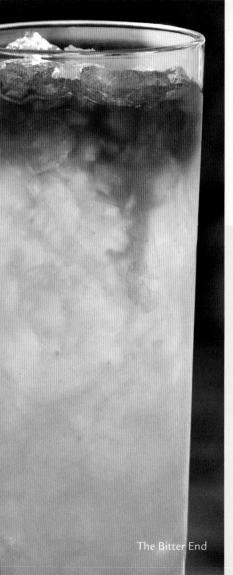

## Burns Night Cap

2 oz. Laphroaig Quarter Cask scotch

½ oz. Benedictine

½ oz. Lillet Blanc

2 dashes Angostura bitters

- Stir all the ingredients with ice.
- Strain into a chilled cocktail glass.

*Notes:*

*The Laphroaig Quarter Cask is a must for this cocktail. The regular 10-year-old bottling is not a substitute.*

## The Bitter End

2 oz. Flor de Caña Aged White 4-year rum

1 oz. grapefruit juice

½ oz. lime juice

½ oz. John D. Taylor's Velvet Falernum

2 dashes Angostura bitters plus up to another ¼ oz. for a float

- Build in a Collins glass using all the ingredients.
- Fill with crushed ice and stir.
- Float an additional 1/4 oz. of Angostura bitters (more or less, according to taste) on top of the drink.

*Notes:*

*To build a cocktail means to combine the ingredients directly in the glass in which it will be served.*

*Falernum is a spiced syrup from Barbados. You can either purchase this ready-made by John D. Taylor or locate one of several recipes published on the web and make it yourself. You may need to tinker with the cocktail recipe if you use a homemade falernum.*

*Don't use an overly large Collins glass for this cocktail. An 8-oz. glass should be plenty.*

# JACKIE PATTERSON

Jackie Patterson?!?! Jackie Patterson?!?! JACKIE PATTERSON?!?!

What, are you kidding me? Jackie Patterson!!!

Did I mention, Jackie Patterson?

Pardon the idiotic exclamations, but it really is the only way to even come close to describing the jubilation that is Jackie Patterson.

Jackie has been bartending with a vengeance for a few years now. Prior to that, she'd been working as a cocktailer, and... ever heard the song by DJ Jazzy Jeff and The Fresh Prince, "I Think I Can Beat Mike Tyson"? Well, Jackie decided that she thought she could win a serious cocktail contest even though she wasn't a boxer...I mean bartender. So she entered the competition and she won. An outraged Mike Tyson came in second with his "Ecstatically Ludicrous Smash" (Killer drink, by the way).

And so, Jackie—by force of will and thrust of talent—circumvented the traditional career arc of a bartender. She was an award-winning bartender before she was a bartender. The heavens fell to earth. Einstein postulated that parallel lines do eventually meet. John Lennon offered a retraction of his line "Children don't do what I have done, I couldn't walk and I tried to run," and replaced it with "Jackie frikkin' rocks!" Such is the power of Jackie (who, incidentally, won the Hawaiian Iron (Wo)man Triathlon before she learned to crawl).

These days, Jackie's made the whirlwind tour of bartending stints at many notable haunts, and left a wake of original cocktails on the menus of such places. She's landed at Heaven's Dog. Heaven's Dog is the type of bar where patrons should just strip nude, walk in with heads bowed, sprawl out on the floor, and release holistically to forces greater than themselves. Surrender to the universe and let it flow in waves over you. That's all I can really say about the place.

And Jackie keeps on winning cocktail competitions, most notably the Marie Brizard competition, which gave her the opportunity to travel to Bordeaux, France, to be pampered and to compete against the whole wide world. She's just got that killer instinct. If the clock's running down, game on the line, and you absolutely need someone to come through with the winning cocktail...pass the rock to Jackie. She won't let you down. She's a true champ-peen.

Update: Jackie's joining up with fellow LCL'ers Dominic Venegas, Matty Eggleston, and Christine D'Abrosca at Martin Cate's Smuggler's Cove.

## Fleur du Monde

1½ oz. Don Julio blanco tequila

¾ oz. Domaine de Canton ginger liqueur

½ oz. Kabinett Riesling

Grapefruit peel, for garnish

↪ Stir all the ingredients with ice for at least 30 seconds.

↪ Strain into a chilled 4½- oz. cocktail glass.

↪ Garnish with the grapefruit peel.

## Catch-22

¾ oz. Batavia Arrack van Oosten

¾ oz. La Gitana manzanilla sherry

¾ oz. Rhum Clément Créole Shrubb

¼ oz. House Chocolate Liquor*

Orange peel, for garnish

↪ Stir all the ingredients with ice for at least 30 seconds.

↪ Strain into a chilled 4½-oz. cocktail glass.

↪ Garnish with the flamed orange peel.

*Notes:*

*This is one of three cocktails in the book that calls for Batavia Arrack. It takes a really skilled bartender to use this odd ingredient and wind up with something yummy. Jackie totally succeeds. I also like this better and better as it warms up and more of the chocolate comes through.*

Catch-22

## Bohemian

1 oz. Bacardi Superior rum

1 oz. Lemon Hart Demerara rum

1 oz. St. Germain elderflower liqueur

½ oz. Licor 43

½ oz. lemon juice

½ oz. lime juice

1 drop absinthe

Lemon peel spiral, for garnish

↷ Shake all the ingredients over ice.

↷ Strain over crushed ice into a highball glass.

↷ Garnish with the lemon peel spiral.

## William Orange

1½ oz. highland single malt scotch

½ oz. Grand Marnier

½ oz. Orgeat*

½ oz. lime juice

1 drop absinthe

1 drop Fee Brothers Whiskey Barrel-Aged bitters

Sprig of mint, for garnish

↷ Shake all the ingredients over ice.

↷ Strain over crushed ice into a rocks glass.

↷ Garnish with the sprig of mint.

*Notes:*

*Jimmy says to use the Grand Marnier 100 (AKA Cuvée du Centenaire) if possible. This is a limited bottling of Grand Marnier that incorporates 25-year-old cognacs.*

William Orange

# JIMMY PATRICK

Jimmy is just the type of bartender we love to feature in Left Coast Libations (as opposed to the other 50 people in this book, who are all nothing but thorns in my freaking side!). Jimmy quietly tends bar and creates cocktails in Sunnyvale, California, just south of San Francisco Bay, slightly north of San Jose. His spot for doing so is The Lion & Compass. The L&C has been around for 25 years, which in Silicon Valley time is more like 300. It is billed as "the premiere dining spot for the high-tech cognescenti [*sic*]." That makes Jimmy's presence all the more appropriate, because not only does he make drinks, he also programs and develops nifty cocktail-themed gizmos. So he speaks the language of the natives.

Anyone know what the hell "cognescenti" means, by the way?

Yes indeed, Jimmy is the creator of the Daily Cocktail gadget, which has been delivering morning temptation to Google users for years now, in the form of drink recipes that Jimmy has deemed most essential. In a related technology, Jimmy has developed the iPhone application, 101 Cocktails. Jimmy describes the app as the "distillation of years of professional bartending experience into a portable iPhone application." In other words, it eschews the tendency to include 48,000 drink recipes and instead selects the 101 that you will actually need in order to a) work behind the bar, b) impress chicks and/or dudes at parties, c) both, d) at the same time.

Jimmy is also very up-front about the fact that this app won't give you slippery nipples or screaming orgasms. But you should buy it anyway. It's available on the iTunes App store. You can always give yourself slippery nipples and screaming orgasms, then load up 101 Cocktails. Sounds like a full evening to me.

In the midst of this technology, let's not forget that Jimmy's true gift is the simple, low-tech trade of welcoming guests to his bar and supplying them with an array of lovely cocktails that suit their tastes. He is widely respected among his peers (from reading Lance Mayhew's blog, I initially thought Jimmy's full name was "The Great Jimmy Patrick"), and his insights and recipes have been published numerous times—look for his excellent and easy to make Jose McGregor in *Food & Wine Cocktails 2008*. That is to say, look for it, memorize it, then put that book down and buy this one instead. After all, Jimmy described the William Orange and Bohemian as "far superior to that lesser drink I gave the fools at *Food & Wine*," and LCL as being "so much more bad-ass than *Food & Wine Cocktails* it ain't even funny." Thanks for the props, Jimmy!

(Note: Mr. Patrick's quotes have been generously provided and scripted by Ted Munat. All rights reserved. Good night.)

# JENNIFER COLLIAU

Jennifer is a spectacular bartender who can be found these days at The Slanted Door, as well as Heaven's Dog. (Yes, there's that name again: see Jon Santer, Erik Adkins, Jackie Patterson, and Lane Ford for further Dog plugging.)

Jennifer has an affection for the pre-Prohibition era. And she seems to have a clear vision of how to create a sensible representation of its glory in this modern age. Step one: create your own line of amazing cocktail ingredients that hearken back to those used before Prohibition. Jennifer has done this in the form of Small Hand Foods. Her line of products includes a Gum Syrup, Pineapple Gum Syrup, Orgeat, and seasonally available Raspberry Gum Syrup and Grenadine. She uses all-natural, highest-quality ingredients, including unrefined sugar (don't even get me started on refined sugar). Most importantly, all her products are delicious. The Orgeat, when tasted alone, seems to enter the mouth like some glorious, supple marble, then an instant later disintegrates, leaving no sticky residue, only aromas of marzipan and orange flowers. These products have been embraced by Bay Area bartenders, who use them to make transcendent reproductions of classic cocktails, as well as brand new creations. Bartenders from other parts of the Left Coast, unable to get Small Hand Foods bottles in their areas, gaze sadly at their Bay Area peers like a child who must learn to play piano while all the other kids play kickball.

Step two: point out that in the pre-Prohibition era, bartenders were...well...all dudes. It sure is fun to play dress up and get out the vests and arm garters and pretend like we're all back in 1902. I mean, I've personally never done that and find the practice a bit disturbing, but I bet it's fun. But visualize with me for a moment: in that nostalgic picture in our inner minds of the old time watering hole, what's the woman behind the bar wearing? There is no woman behind the bar, is there? Maybe we need to reconcile that.

What's Jennifer going to be doing about that? Well, I hear she's training to be a boxer, so apparently she's just going to start beating the crap out of people. Excellent plan. She'll also keep making outstanding drinks at some of the city's best bars, increase the distribution of her heavenly Small Hand Foods, and think up new ideas for more cocktail ingredients that will surely heighten not only her own drinks, but the drinks of her peers as well.

And here ends my own twisted interpretation of Jennifer's plan to bring sunshine to all of our lives.

## Brace

1½ oz. pisco

1 oz. Lime-Whey Mixture*

½ oz. manzanilla sherry

½ oz. Cointreau

½ oz. Simple Syrup*

3 dashes The Bitter Truth celery bitters

Orange peel, for garnish

↪ Shake all the ingredients vigorously over ice.

↪ Double-strain into a chilled coupe.

↪ Garnish with the orange peel.

Reunion Cooler

## Reunion Cooler

½ oz. (by volume, not weight) pink peppercorns

Four 1 inch chunks ripe pineapple

Two 1 x 8 inch strips of grapefruit peel (no pith)

1 oz. blanco tequila

½ oz. lime juice

1 barspoon agave nectar

↪ Crush the peppercorns in the bottom of a mixing glass with a muddler.

↪ Add the pineapple and one of the grapefruit peels; muddle thoroughly.

↪ Add the tequila, lime juice, and agave nectar, fill with ice, and shake thoroughly.

↪ Strain through a julep strainer into a double Old Fashioned glass filled with fresh ice.

↪ Garnish with the remaining grapefruit peel.

*Notes:*

*Jennifer prefers El Tesoro or Don Julio tequila for this cocktail.*

*Measure the peppercorns by filling a ½ oz. jigger with them.*

*Do NOT double-strain this cocktail. There should be flecks of pink from the peppercorns in it.*

*Jennifer makes a horse's neck with the grapefruit peel. This is a long wide peel that can either be wrapped up tightly, like a kind of flower, and set atop the ice in the drink, or loosely coiled inside the glass to form a collar at the top, which is how it's done for a crusta.*

# RYAN FITZGERALD

Ryan "Fitzy" Fitzgerald is a former Australian Rules football player for...hang on a minute. Whoops. Wrong Ryan Fitzgerald. I think. Let me re-check...yeah. Totally the wrong Ryan Fitzgerald. Let's start over again...

Ryan "Don't You Dare Call Me 'Fitzy'" Fitzgerald is a bartender. I know because he's in my book, and it's about bartenders, not Australian Rules football players. I also know because I've witnessed him tend bar myself, which he does with considerable skill and panache at Beretta these days. Former slinging posts of his include Bourbon & Branch and Tres Agaves. Ryan professes a love of tequila, which must have flourished during his years at Tres Agaves, and still loves working with it (or drinking it—even better). But he's also capable of dreaming up something simple, elegant, and rye-based such as the Rocky Mountain Monkberry. That's what you call "versatile." Hell, he probably could be an Australian Rules football player if he wanted to. It might actually help him at work. Beretta tends to be very crowded, and controlled violence is sometimes needed to make your way around the place.

Trivia question: What do Jim Romdall, Jay Kuehner, Ryan Fitzgerald, and I all have in common? Answer: we all studied film, and now we all drink. Fellas, let's make a movie...and drink.

Ryan, in addition to tending bar, has developed a web site, ihatecocktails.com. The web site is loosely based on the shirt of the same name, which is in turn loosely based upon Ryan's torso at most well-attended cocktail events in the country. Many laugh and suppose this is an ironic statement on Ryan's part. It isn't. He hates cocktails. I've seen him whipping them around with barspoons and shaking them over his shoulder like they was talking about his mama.

As of this writing, ihatecocktails.com consists of a few pictures of Ryan wearing his shirt and the words, "Coming Soon..." Color me intrigued! In the mean time, the pictures of Ryan in his "I Hate Cocktails" shirt are worth the visit. When visiting, I recommend...the pictures of Ryan in his "I Hate Cocktails shirt." And remember: no irony. Go see Ryan at Beretta, and you'll see that he's totally sincere. The most sincere bartender in North America, I'd say. The sincerity comes through in every amazing cocktail he makes, even if he does hate them.

## Rocky Mountain Monkberry

2 oz. Rittenhouse 100-proof rye

½ oz. Benedictine

½ oz. Leopold Brothers Rocky Mountain blackberry liqueur

Broad lime twist, for garnish

- Stir all the ingredients with ice.
- Strain into a chilled, small cocktail glass.
- Garnish with the broad lime twist.

*Notes:*

*The lime peel garnish really matters in this drink, the tart aromatic oil adding just the right counterpoint to the sweetness of the liqueur. Be sure to twist it over the drink to express the oils before serving.*

Rocky Mountain Monkberry

## Il Terzo

1½ oz. Dried Apricot–infused Peruvian pisco*

1 oz. grapefruit juice

½ oz. Los Danzantes reposado mezcal

½ oz. Dimmi liqueur

½ oz. lemon juice

½ oz. 1:1 Honey Syrup*

Slice of fresh apricot, for garnish

- Shake all the ingredients over ice.
- Double-strain into a cocktail glass.
- Garnish with the apricot slice on the side of the glass.

*Notes:*

*Rumor has it Los Danzantes mezcal may soon be rebranded, so it may now be called something else. It will still be distributed by Craft Distillers.*

*Dimmi used to be called Veloce di Milano.*

## The General Lee

1½ oz. Wild Turkey 101-proof rye

½ oz. lemon juice

½ oz. Simple Syrup*

1 tbsp. Kumquat Marmalade*

3 dashes Peychaud's bitters

➷ Shake all the ingredients over ice.

➷ Strain over fresh ice into a rocks glass.

## The Bull on the Hill

1½ oz. Lustau dry oloroso sherry

1 oz. Plymouth gin

½ oz. 2:1 Demerara Syrup*

½ tbsp. green Chartreuse

⅛ oz. orange juice

⅛ oz. lemon juice

2 drops Angostura bitters

2 drops Dried Chili–Infused Orange Bitters*

2 drops veal demi-glace

Orange peel, for garnish

➷ Shake all the ingredients over ice.

➷ Strain into a chilled cocktail glass.

➷ Squeeze the orange peel over the top to express the oils and discard the peel.

Notes:

*Demi-glace is a very concentrated reduction of meat and other flavorings—far more concentrated than a normal stock. Veal demi-glace may be bought premade. Matty recommends the More Than Gourmet brand available at some Whole Foods markets. You may also find it at Williams-Sonoma and Sur La Table stores.*

*I have also experimented with a shortcut that involves substituting two drops of Bragg Liquid Aminos in place of the demi-glace.*

The General Lee

# MATTY EGGLESTON

It is a well known fact that Matty Eggleston drank the devil's beer for nothin' and then he stole his song.

Hard to believe really...he seems like such a nice young man.

Matty is easily one of Los Angeles' most respected bartenders, having worked at many of the city's best places, and also having made significant contributions to the bartending community. For the past few years he did wondrous deeds at The Hungry Cat, located at Sunset and Vine. Matty's got some Hollywood in him (in a good way), so it makes sense that he would have stood in its heart while establishing himself in the show business known as bartending. A quick look at The Hungry Cat's cocktail menu reveals not a single drink without some sort of fresh ingredient, whether it be tomatoes or cucumbers or watermelon or what have you (the what have you is best in spring). This is an outgrowth both of Matty's philosophy of cocktails and the bounty of produce locally available in Southern California.

Over time, Matty developed a tendency to work at The Varnish, which is fast becoming LA's answer to Heaven's Dog of San Francisco in terms of bartending star power. If you care to keep score, Eric Alperin, Chris Ojeda, Marcos Tello, and Matty are all there at some time or another. Perhaps they should simply start holding their Guild meetings there.

Speaking of the Guild (seamless transition baby, how you like that?), Matty finds himself treasurer of the newly revived Southern California chapter of the USBG. The chapter is working to help elevate the craft in its part of the world, to prepare bartenders to become USBG-certified and get scholarships for the ever-so-pricey Beverage Alcohol Resource (BAR) program, and to throw me a birthday party!

Unfortunately, just as the birthday party concept was becoming a reality, Matty up and moved to San Francisco, embezzling a substantial sum of the Guild's money. OK I made the embezzlement story up. Actually the whole birthday party thing was a lie too. One lie leads to another. You can look it up. It's in the bible. OK it's not. Or it is, but not in so many words.

Truth is...Matty. Matty is the truth. And the other truth is...Matty did move to San Francisco, and he started working at Smuggler's Cove, like a lot of other LCL'ers. If you are in fact the devil, and you are looking for your song and a free beer, this is where you will find Matty. Honest.

## Solera

1¾ oz. Santa Teresa 1796 rum

1¼ oz. oloroso sherry

½ oz. John D. Taylor's Velvet Falernum

Orange peel, for garnish

- Stir all the ingredients with ice.
- Strain into a cocktail glass.
- Garnish with the orange peel.

*Notes:*

*Oloroso sherries can vary quite a bit in terms of dryness. I used Lustau East India sherry, which is pretty sweet, and it dominated the cocktail. You may want to try a drier one.*

*Falernum is a spiced syrup from Barbados. You can either purchase this ready-made by John D. Taylor or locate one of several recipes published on the web and make it yourself. You may need to tinker with the cocktail recipe if you use a homemade falernum.*

## Stallion

2 oz. Beefeater gin

1 oz. Barolo Chinato

½ oz. Senior Curaçao de Curaçao (white)

1 dash of Angostura orange bitters

- Stir all the ingredients with ice.
- Strain into a cocktail glass.

*Notes:*

*When I first proofed this recipe I asked Dominic if there was a garnish and he replied: "NO garnish, it bucks on its own."*

*Barolo Chinato is a regional Italian specialty made by infusing Barolo wine with quinine, spices, and herbs and then aging the results in oak for at least five years. It is based on the work of the nineteenth-century pharmacist Giuseppe Cappellano to create a unique digestif.*

Stallion

# DOMINIC VENEGAS

Some bartenders have lists of bars they've worked at. Dominic might have a list of bars he hasn't worked at. And listening to Dominic tell his story in the bartending field is somewhat like hearing the modern history of the industry itself. The bartenders featured in this book, along with countless others around the world, hope that the public will come to perceive bartending as a profession, not a job, and that the proper prestige and respect will follow. Five minutes listening to Dominic speak about his career is all that's really required for the listener's paradigm to be shifted in this direction. Dominic himself relates stories of telling people he is a bartender, and being asked what he wants to do after he's done with that. He shrugs and smiles and says, "You know what, I kind of like bartending. I think I might just keep doing it."

Many of the bars featured in this book—Bourbon & Branch, Cantina, and Range—have Dominic's fingerprints on them. He's taken quite a liking to designing and implementing bar programs, shepherding their opening and initial growth stages, then moving on to the next challenge. The most recently completed project would be Gitane, a beautiful spot in a little alleyway that feels like a portal to another land and time.

Creating a bar program involves not only menu design and spirit selection, but also the layout of the bar itself, not to mention shaping the philosophy and the culture of an establishment. Dominic does this from the perspective of a bartender, bearing in mind what will enable the folks working at the bar to best do their job. This might seem like a given, but you would be surprised how often this is not taken into consideration when a bar is designed by those who never had to work one.

Dominic also works as the spirits buyer for John Walker, the legendary liquor store that opened its doors the day Prohibition was repealed. For this wide-eyed boy from the control state of Washington, bearing witness to Dominic's selection was akin to my first trip to Disney World. I'd never seen most of the bottles lining the shelves, yet Dominic knew everything about everything. Were I a man of greater faith, I might have thought him a spirit god. Perhaps this will indeed turn out to be the case.

UPDATE: Dominic's latest bartending gig is at Smuggler's Cove, a new bar from Tiki legend Martin Cate (one of many brilliant bartenders NOT in this book...perhaps the next volume?). Smuggler's Cove features "traditional drinks of the Caribbean Islands, classic libations of Prohibition-era Havana, and exotic cocktails from legendary Tiki bars." Everyone's very excited about this bar, and with Dominic on board, well...frankly, my nipples are hard. All you young bartenders out there, check Dominic out. He's firmly established as one of the best but is still looking for ways to expand his repertoire. Dominic's going to do Tiki...I'll be damned!

# DUGGAN MCDONNELL

Among many other accomplishments, Duggan holds an MFA in Writing from the University of San Francisco. His hifalutin' degree has this writer intimidated. I'm going to have to write fancy here. Please forgive me...

Duggan is totally rad and kicks ass as a bartender, and his bar, Cantina, is really awesome. In fact, he bartends so good that the people at Tales of The Cocktail, back in 2007, were all, "You're nominated for Best Mixologist of the year!" And Duggan was all like, "Sa-weet!" And they were all like, "Yep." And then in 2008 they were all, "Check it out dude, we're nominating you again!" And he was all, "No!" And they were all, "Yep!" And then *Food & Wine* magazine was all, "You're a leader of the American cocktail revolution!" And Duggan was all, "I know!" And then San Francisco Rising Stars (starchefs.com), *Vogue, Maxim, Cheers!, Time, The New York Times, Food Arts*, and *The Wall Street Journal* were all "Hold up! We wanna show Duggan some love too!" And Duggan was all, "Easy kids, there's enough of me to go around!" And there totally was!

OK, I simply can't keep up the intellectual banter anymore. I hope Mr. McDonnell is dutifully impressed.

I also hope you got out of the above diatribe that Duggan is one of the most celebrated, honored, and awarded bartenders in the world. He co-owns his own bar, Cantina, in San Francisco. Cantina is pretty much one big party. It's an excellent example of a place that serves creative and sophisticated cocktails (and pitchers!) while at the same time offering a wild and carefree time. In that way, it's actually an accurate reflection of its owner.

When not orchestrating the frenzy at Cantina, Duggan runs his own cocktail consulting company, Liquid Think Tank, LLC; judges at the Los Angeles International Wine & Spirits Competition; and travels all over the world to tour distilleries, breweries, and wineries. Tough life, eh? He also writes articles for *SOMA, Imbibe*, and chow.com.

Most important to know though is this portion of Duggan's bio: he believes wholly in the Beverage Lifestyle. Voltaire said that as long as people believe in absurdities, they will continue to commit atrocities. Nothing absurd about the Beverage Lifestyle, which explains why Duggan commits nothing but acts of love and drink recipes to memory. Voltaire, if you're reading this, you totally should check out Cantina.

## The Misdemeanor

2 pieces diced pineapple

1 thin slice of Serrano chili

½ oz. agave nectar

2 oz. Partida blanco tequila

1 oz. lime juice

½ oz. green Chartreuse

☙ Muddle the pineapple, chili, and agave nectar in a mixing glass.

☙ Add the remaining ingredients and ice, and shake vigorously.

☙ Strain into a highball glass.

*Notes:*

Duggan writes: *"I chose to do the two cocktails with chilies so that one's mise-en-place could be minimalized. I always use serrano chilies and slice them width-wise in thin slices, and frankly let the gods of heat rule from there. Sometimes, shit is hot! Sometimes, it ain't."*

Laughing Buddha

## Laughing Buddha

3 small pieces of fresh ginger, plus 1 slice fresh ginger for garnish

1 thin slice of Serrano chili

2 oz. Hangar One Buddha's Hand vodka

1 oz. lime juice

½ oz. Five Spice–Infused Agave Nectar*

Barrit's Ginger Beer

Cucumber wedge, for garnish

☙ Muddle the ginger and chili in a mixing glass.

☙ Add all the remaining ingredients, except for the ginger beer and ice.

☙ Shake vigorously.

☙ Strain into a highball glass, simultaneously pouring enough of the ginger beer to fill the glass.

☙ Garnish with the ginger slice and cucumber wedge.

*Notes:*

Duggan is very specific that the ginger beer is to be poured into the glass simultaneously with the cocktail and not added afterwards to top it off.

# JON SANTER

I've heard people describe Jon as both "The Ice King" and "The Wizard of Dilution." Let's face it, you got Jon Santer behind the bar, you're about three elves and a wicked queen away from a fairy tale.

While there's no doubt Jon has skills with ice and can preach with authority on the methods for properly diluting a cocktail, such labels have been issued with a subtle sense of irony, as their grandeur runs contrary to the actual humility with which he conducts himself—both behind the bar and away from it.

Jon has been bartending in the Bay Area for many years. He was an integral part of the crew that opened Bourbon & Branch, and later did the same at Beretta. He recently helped open Heaven's Dog, a bar that the reader is guaranteed to grow tired of hearing about if reading this book from cover to cover.

It seems as though Jon is rewarded by the challenge of opening a new place, establishing the groundwork and environment in order to get the momentum going in the proper direction, and then ushering it ever so gently to its independence. So in addition to the aforementioned nicknames, let's add to them, "The Human Training Wheels." One thing by which the discerning drinker will no doubt be impressed when bar hopping in San Francisco is the consistent results you can count on nightly at the city's best bars. Certainly there are some bartenders, such as the ones in this book, who take things to a new level of creativity and skill. But one of the signs of a truly great cocktail program is consistently excellent drinks, no matter which bartender happens to be working. The efforts of people like Jon (and many others included in this book as well) to lay a sound foundation play a huge role in making this happen.

Jon is also U.S. National Brand Ambassador for Martin Miller's Gin, director of the Beverage Academy in San Francisco, and served as president of the San Francisco chapter of the United States Bartenders' Guild from 2007 to 2009. Apart from that, he really serves no role in the bartending community. He's your typical slacker.

It is through his work with Martin Miller's that I came to work with Jon, putting together cocktail events in Seattle. I've learned a lot from him, about bartending, event preparation, and life's rich pageant. We all really like Jon up here in the Northwest, and we try to come up with excuses to get him up our way so we can roll out our soggy, mossy red carpets.

If you happen to see Jon hanging out, and you feel an overwhelming urge to pick his brain about all things spirit and cocktail, this is understandable. After all, the man is a trove of knowledge on the subject. But do me a favor? Leave the poor guy alone about it already. He works hard. Maybe he'd rather talk about something else, like ponies or princesses, or whatever. Deal? Thanks.

## The Revolver

2 oz. Bulleit Bourbon

½ oz. Tia Maria

1 dash Fee Brothers orange bitters

1 dash Regan's orange bitters

Orange peel, for garnish

*Notes:*

*By "large ice" Jon refers to KOLD-DRAFT cubes or chunks of ice that have been hewn from a large block using an ice pick or a saw.*

- ✐ Combine all the ingredients in a frozen mixing glass.
- ✐ Stir with large ice until chilled.
- ✐ Strain into a frozen cocktail glass (yield is 4½ oz. when properly diluted).
- ✐ Flame a disc of orange peel with a wooden match about 5 inches off the top of the cocktail and then drop in the peel.

## Dragon Variation

1½ oz. Martin Miller's Westbourne Strength gin

½ oz. Dolin blanc vermouth

10 drops Thai Chili Tincture*

- ✐ Combine all the ingredients in a frozen mixing glass.
- ✐ Stir with large ice until chilled.
- ✐ Strain into a frozen cocktail glass (yield is 4 oz. when properly diluted).

*Notes:*

*Of all the LCL bartenders, Jon is most precise about his drink dilution and chilling. The length of time it takes to attain the indicated yield of these cocktails will depend greatly on the ice you are using. Commercial bag and homemade ice will melt faster than "benchmark" KOLD-DRAFT cubes or a hewn chunk.*

*Also note that the Dolin blanc is not to be confused with the Dolin dry vermouth.*

The Revolver

## Chartreuse Swizzle

1¼ oz. green Chartreuse

½ oz. John D. Taylor's Velvet Falernum

1 oz. pineapple juice

Juice of ½ lime

Lime wheel, for garnish

Sprig of mint, for garnish

- Swizzle all the ingredients with crushed ice (or shake with ice and strain over crushed ice) in a tall glass.
- Garnish with the lime wheel and mint sprig.

*Notes:*

*Swizzling refers to mixing a cocktail with a specialized tool called...a swizzle stick. These have made something of a resurgence recently and you may be able to purchase them at some liquor stores and through the Internet.*

*Falernum is a spiced syrup from Barbados. You can either purchase this ready-made by John D. Taylor or locate one of several recipes published on the web and make it yourself. You may need to tinker with the cocktail recipe if you use a homemade falernum.*

## English Breakfast

1½ oz. Earl Grey Tea–Infused No. 209 gin*

¾ oz. Grand Marnier

¾ oz. fresh lemon juice

1 barspoon orange marmalade

1 egg white

Qi black tea liqueur, for garnish

- Dry shake all the ingredients.
- Add ice and shake again.
- Double-strain into a port glass.
- Spray top of drink with the Qi black tea liqueur using a Misto pump.

*Notes:*

*Misto pumps, which allow you to turn most liquids into a fine aerosol, can be purchased at stores specializing in kitchen equipment.*

Chartreuse Swizzle

# MARCO DIONYSOS

Marco has been bartending for, gosh, I'd say about 15 years or so? He's widely thought of as one of the most masterful and influential bartenders in the Bay Area, and the list of spots he's delivered from includes Stars, Enrico's, Moose's, Vesuvio's, Harry Denton's Starlight Room, Absinthe, Tres Agaves, and Clock Bar.

He used to live and work in Portland, where, according to Marco, he practiced "Mai Tai Chi," (which of course is not to be confused with Mai Taikido or Mai Taekwondo). He left in 1996, and soon after was named by *Willamette Week* as "Best Bartender (Who Left Town)." This is, naturally, a considerably greater honor than being named "Best Bartender We Wish Would Leave Town." Why did Marco leave town? Probably on the run from Johnny Law.

Since relocating to the Bay Area, Marco has emerged as a bona fide star, having been featured in *GQ, Playboy, Wine Spectator*, the *San Francisco Chronicle*, and various in-flight magazines. I would imagine he was featured as a result of his bartending prowess, but it's always possible they just wanted to run a photo of that handsome puss of his. Marco has also represented the U.S. at the Beefeater International Bartenders Competition in Barcelona, the Pan-American Cocktail Competitions in Puerto Rico and Venezuela, the Domaine de Canton Bartender of the Year Competition in French St. Martin, and in the 2008 Olympics, where he won silver in the 100-meter freestyle muddle.

Marco recently ended his tenure at Clock Bar, and as of this writing is contemplating what to do next. In case he's considering a return to the Pacific Northwest, let me state for the record right here: he can crash on my couch until he gets situated. Clock Bar was a beautiful space, replete with all the stock and tools and perks any dedicated bartender could dream of, yet Marco walked away from it. Why would he do such a thing? Probably on the run from Johnny Law again. He is, after all, the Clyde Barrow of the cocktail world—from the law-breaking to the dapper dress. Let's hope he takes me up on the offer and swings through Seattle one step ahead of The Man. I'd join him. I could use a good Bonnie and Clyde experience. I've already got my sequined cloche hat picked out.

Cocktail refugees…I like the sound of that.

Keep your eyes peeled and your ears to the ground. The mysterious Marco is bound to re-surface somewhere.

(Update: Marco didn't get word of my couch offer and re-surfaced at Rye in San Francisco.)

# ERIK ADKINS

Many bartenders have told me that Erik Adkins is the best bartender they have ever witnessed.

Sorry, I have no smart-ass line to add to this one. The fact is, some of the best in the business believe this man is the best in the business. Their reverence stems not only from his creativity, legendary attention to detail, and perfectionism (Erik is purported to often make a drink 100 times or more, tinkering each time, until he believes it's perfect...only then is it ready to be put on the menu), but most of all from his presence behind a bar. It is a commanding presence, and he has the ability to welcome everyone who enters his establishment, infusing them with his enthusiasm.

That's an often overlooked skill for a bartender. We've probably all had the experience of being new to cocktails, or new to a particular place for cocktails, and feeling ostracized—as if violating some secret club when we enter, greeted by cold stares and rolled eyes. (That's how my brother and I used to keep the crowds away at Vessel.) Erik will have none of that.

Erik used to pour beers alongside fellow LCL'er and good pal Daniel Shoemaker. When I asked Erik which of them became interested in cocktails first, he quickly declared that it was Daniel. Daniel, when told of this, would wittily retort, "Liar, liar, pants. On. FIRE!" Daniel further reports that Erik was, in fact, into cocktails well before he ever was, and when Daniel was preparing to open Teardrop Lounge, he called Erik multiple times each day seeking advice, which was always lengthily provided.

So the moral to the story is: Erik is a damn liar. Don't believe a word he says.

Erik is the mastermind behind the cocktail programs at The Slanted Door and Flora. The Slanted Door is a spectacle to behold: a massive, glistening place along San Francisco's waterfront where expertly made cocktails using housemade bitters and tinctures and syrups are churned out, seemingly at a rate of 100 per minute. Flora is the beautiful Art Deco spot in downtown Oakland where Erik developed the bar program and continues to consult. Glimpses of Flora can be seen on every other page of this book, sitting pretty behind the cocktails.

Erik's primary vocation at this point is managing the bar at Heaven's Dog. Aren't we all sick of hearing about Heaven's Dog at this point? No, me neither. Simply put, Heaven's Dog is a bar where you can go any time it happens to be open and find yourself being served by one of the best bartenders in the world. It's also the spot to catch Mr. Adkins at work behind the bar. If you trust the opinions of folks such as Jon Santer, Daniel Shoemaker, and many others, that's something not to be missed.

Just remember. He is, in fact, a liar.

## Carter Beats the Devil

2 oz. reposado tequila

1 oz. lime juice

½ oz. agave nectar

¼ oz. smoky mezcal

10 drops Thai Chili Tincture*

Lime spiral, for garnish

☙ Shake all the ingredients over ice.

☙ Strain into a cocktail glass.

☙ Garnish with the lime spiral.

*Notes:*

*Erik prefers using the Del Maguey 'Minero' mezcal for this cocktail.*

## Filibuster

1½ oz. rye

¾ oz. lemon juice

½ oz. grade B maple syrup

1 egg white

Angostura bitters, for garnish

☙ Dry shake all the ingredients.

☙ Add ice and shake again.

☙ Strain into a chilled cocktail glass.

☙ Garnish with a few drops of Angostura bitters in the froth. Use a wooden toothpick to "draw" the drops into a fanciful design.

*Notes:*

*Erik pointed out that the version of this recipe published by Food & Wine magazine incorrectly called for ¼ oz. of maple syrup, resulting in a cocktail that was way too tart.*

*The froth on this cocktail must be really thick or the bitters will disperse it, leaving unsightly holes in the top. See the appendix on homemade ingredients for tips on frothing egg whites. You must become the master of the egg whites before attempting this one.*

PORTLAND, Oregon is a great walking town, and therefore it is only appropriate that all of the city's finest bars lie within easy walking distance of each other. Clyde Common, ten01, 50 Plates, and Teardrop Lounge very considerately built themselves within short Portland blocks of one another, making for one of the most divinely sophisticated bar crawls on earth.

Update: Beaker and Flask, featuring Dave Shenaut, opened over on the east side...but you can still walk there. Just don't be a wuss already.

Update: Evan Zimmerman left Teardrop and opened Laurelhurst Market over on East 28th Street — yeah, for that you might need a bike or a cab.

Update: Lance Mayhew is now over at Branch — Holy crap, that's way over on Alberta. OK, we're looking at some serious cab fares now.

Update: Amazing bars are popping up all over Portland. And reminder: This book features bartenders from Corvallis, 85 miles away from Portland.

OK, so the cocktail scene here obviously is expanding with no consideration for the convenience of the cocktail completist. But we simply must respond to the challenge. So go to Oregon regardless of the degree of difficulty. Bring your walking shoes, your bicycle, some cab money, a Learjet, and a bullet train. You'll do just fine.

# PORTLAND

Ten01

# DANIEL SHOEMAKER

By Daniel's own admission, prior to developing a fascination with cocktails he spent years pouring something called "beer," and not even for use in cocktails! He'd just pour the beer into a glass and maybe describe the beer to some beer-soaked souse too busy drinking tons of beer to pay attention to what Daniel was saying about his beer. Beer!

This sordid chapter of his life apparently took place in San Francisco, and occurred before a switch was flipped and Daniel became the great tincture/bitters/cocktail savant of the West: not the most catchy title, but it is accurate. Realizing there's really no interest in cocktails in San Francisco, Daniel moved to the real cocktail Mecca of the western world, Portland, Oregon, and opened Teardrop Lounge.

A day will come in the near future when Daniel will need to expand Teardrop to make room for the ever-growing collection of housemade bitters, liqueurs, tonics, etc. It's a truly breathtaking array of exquisitely made ingredients that can't be had anywhere else in the world, and all are deftly incorporated into delicious cocktails.

It's also kind of scary. Daniel says it's his OCD kicking into overdrive, but there's something far more intense and sinister going on. There's a point when it stops feeling like an impressive display of housemade ingredients and begins feeling like a revolutionary, Kaczynski-esque manifesto. We're all a little worried about him, actually.

Life has changed for Daniel since he shed microbrews and found cocktails. He now will pour a cocktail into a glass and maybe describe the cocktail to some cocktail-soaked souse too busy drinking cocktails to pay attention to what Daniel is saying about his cocktail. (I was fortunate enough to witness one gentleman patron of Teardrop Lounge who, after watching Daniel put a dash of bitters into his cocktail, threatened to kick his ass if he ever tried slipping hot sauce into his drink again...welcome to Portland, Daniel!)

When Daniel isn't converting the patrons of his abode (or pissing them off with his hot-sauce pranks), he's helping to run the fabulous Oregon Bartenders Guild and...well, making housemade ingredients...that's about all he does as far as I can tell. He claims he sleeps, though no one has ever witnessed it. Seriously. We are really worried about him.

## Sandcastles in the Sky

1 long strip lemon peel

1 long strip orange peel

1½ oz. Glenfarclas 12-year-old scotch

¾ oz. Floc de Gascogne

½ oz. Benedictine

1 dash Marteau absinthe

10 drops Costus Root Bitters*

&#x25B9; Cut the lemon and orange peel strips over a mixing glass and drop them in.

&#x25B9; Lightly press the peels with the back of a mixing spoon or muddler to express the oils.

&#x25B9; Add all the remaining ingredients to the mixing glass.

&#x25B9; Stir with ice for 30 seconds.

&#x25B9; Strain into a cocktail glass.

*Notes:*

*Floc de Gascogne is a regional aperitif made in the Armagnac and Côtes de Gascogne regions of France from ⅓ armagnac and ⅔ fresh grape juice, both from the same vineyard. Daniel says Pineau de Charentes (another French aperitif) may be used as a substitute.*

## Illuminations

1½ oz. El Tesoro reposado tequila

1 oz. lemon juice

¾ oz. Lustau East India sherry

½ oz. grade B maple syrup

½ oz. egg white

&#x25B9; Dry shake all the ingredients for 20 seconds.

&#x25B9; Add ice, shake for an additional 6 seconds.

&#x25B9; Double-strain into a champagne coupe.

*Notes:*

*Daniel says he prefers to use the whites of farm-fresh brown eggs for this cocktail.*

Illuminations

## Smoke Signals

1½ oz. Tennessee whiskey

1 oz. manzanilla sherry

¾ oz Pecan Syrup*

½ oz. lemon juice

1 dash The Bitter Truth Jerry Thomas' Own Decanter bitters

Smoked Ice*

- Combine all the ingredients except smoked ice in a shaker with (not smoked) ice.
- Shake hard.
- Double-strain over a 2" by 2" block of the smoked ice in an Old Fashioned glass.

## Morning Bell

1 oz. Glenmorangie Nectar d'Or single malt scotch

1 oz. Sauternes

1 oz. calvados

2 dashes Peychaud's bitters

- Stir all the ingredients with ice until thoroughly chilled.
- Strain into a cognac snifter.

*Notes:*

*Evan says you may try substituting any highly botrytised wine in place of the Sauternes in this cocktail, albeit to different effects.*

Smoke Signals

# EVAN ZIMMERMAN

I don't know where the hell Evan Zimmerman comes from and I don't care.

OK, he did tell me once he used to live in Charleston, South Carolina. Went to something called "college" there.

But I don't care. In my life, he appeared one night at Teardrop Lounge, wildly darting about, whipping drinks together like the Mad Hatter serving tea for the big un-birthday. And I thought to myself, "Who's the new guy?" Always ready with the witticisms, am I.

A bit later, Daniel Shoemaker came over. I informed him I was writing a book, and that he would be in it, and asked who else should be included. Daniel nodded in the direction of Evan and explained to me that the new guy was the future of cocktails in Portland—the next great thing. I asked him what about the other guy over there, gesturing towards Jeffrey Morgenthaler. "Hack," said Shoemaker.

I love making up stories about bartenders.

But the first part—the part about Evan—is true. No really. And Daniel was right. Evan's a tornado behind the bar. And creative, wild, borderline insane shit flies in every direction from where he stands. For the love of God, the man's drink in this book calls for smoked ice. Do you have any idea how far gone from reality a person has to be to conceive of smoking ice? I was a teenager once, and I tried smoking just about everything... but never ice.

The bad news is that Evan is no longer fulfilling the prophecy of Shoemaker at Teardrop Lounge. The good news is that he's now heading up the bar at Laurelhurst Market. Laurelhurst is a restaurant whose renderings of meat in various forms have sent ripples and quivers of excitement up and down the Pacific Northwest, entrancing the most bloodthirsty carnivores of the area. And from this hallowed ground Evan is, well, smoking things, making his own tinctures, tonics, and infusions, and being a general menace to society.

Making one's own tinctures, tonics, and infusions? That's what they do at Teardrop Lounge! And Evan could be there doing it with them. But now he's off doing it somewhere else. It's what we in the cocktail industry call "spreading the virus." The fine art of cocktails is somewhat like zombie-ism when you think of it. Once it bites you, you become one, and off you go, slowly staggering up into the hills, looking for someone else to infect.

Wait, wasn't I talking about Evan? Evan is gifted with the drinks and is a spectacle to behold behind the bar. Find this man. Just don't let him bite you.

# KELLEY SWENSON

Years ago I had a job working the counter at a burrito place on Bainbridge Island, Washington. It was the best job I've ever had. I loved my customers and the people I worked with and I got free burritos. The place was next door to a restaurant and bar called Café Nola, with which it shared a patio. Turns out, on the other side of the wall from me, Kelley Swenson was tending bar, learning a craft that he would soon take to a rarefied level. But we never met.

Many years later I sat down at the bar at ten01, an excellent Portland restaurant and bar where Kelley is now bartender and Spirits Director, and opened my mouth and pretended to be a baby sparrow. Just a thing I like to do at bars. Kelley immediately blew me away with his friendliness, his calm demeanor behind the bar, and his exquisitely conceived and constructed cocktails. We eventually pieced together our respective pasts, deduced we'd been neighbors, and I somberly reflected on all the Bainbridge Island happy hours that could have been, but never were.

Kelley's got the resiliency and savvy to track down unusual spirits (Oregon is yet another "control state," wherein the availability of booze is dictated by the state bureaucracy), and the knowledge and creativity to know how to use them once he's got them. He also embraces the trend toward the use of fresh, seasonal ingredients and collaborating with the kitchen. Basically, if you want a boozy old school drink, Kelley can make you that. You want something with fresh juices and herbs, he can do that too. Glance over at the drinks he contributed to this book...eh? Eh? One of each type right?

Kelley's not a self-promoting type of fella. He's just a humble man who is very good at what he does. But that isn't to say he lacks ambition or interest in elevating his craft through means other than working a shift at his bar. He seems to be continually hosting cocktail-themed events around Portland—often co-hosting with Beaker & Flask bartender Timothy Davey. In recent months, this has included an interactive course on rum along with rum god Ed Hamilton, and a multi-course dinner pairing food with Irish Whiskeys and Porters.

Something one might note about these events is that they are aimed not at promoting Kelley, but at promoting the possibilities and potential of spirits and cocktails as a culinary art and community hitching post. And since he stubbornly refuses to self-promote, let us, the Left Coast Libations' Mob, state for the record: Kelley is one of the absolute finest bartenders on the Left Coast, and a true gentleman. Make it a point to seek him out (and get some truffle fries while you're there).

Celeriac

## Toto

¾ oz. El Jimador reposado tequila

¾ oz. green Chartreuse

¾ oz. Cynar

Lemon twist, for garnish

- Stir all the ingredients with ice.
- Strain into a cocktail glass.
- Garnish with the lemon twist.

*Notes:*

*Kelley says you may also use Cazadores reposado tequila in this cocktail.*

## Celeriac

2 oz. gin

¾ oz. pineapple juice

¾ oz. lemon juice

½ oz. 2:1 Simple Syrup*

4 dashes The Bitter Truth celery bitters

1 egg white

- Dry shake all the ingredients without ice.
- Add ice and shake some more.
- Double-strain into a large cocktail glass or champagne coupe.
- Optional but recommended: pour some celery bitters in an atomizer or Misto pump. Spray a mist of the bitters across the top of the drink to finish.

*Notes:*

*Follow Kelley's advice and finish this cocktail with the celery bitters mist.*

# LANCE MAYHEW

Lance Mayhew is just your average ordinary guy who used to sling Long Islands at Stuart Anderson's Black Angus Fun Bar before rocking Hennessy and brandishing bottles of Galliano like baseball bats at California's finest hip hop clubs. Somewhere along the way he developed a love of classic cocktails and became one of the Northwest's best bartenders and co-founder of the Oregon Bartenders Guild and to this day professes an affection for Dostoevskian Anarchists.

The individual elements of this background may seem disparate, but so might the ingredients of your average ordinary cocktail. And Lance, like a cocktail, makes it all work together in a pleasing way that one probably wouldn't have anticipated.

Lance was working the bar at 50 Plates in Portland, but the time came for him to move over to Beaker & Flask alongside owner and bartending legend Kevin Ludwig (some of us have a theory that Kevin Ludwig is actually a fictional character invented by Lance, but that's a book unto itself). Lance has most recently started working at Branch, a whiskey bar in the Alberta neighborhood—a neighborhood that a crusty old former Portland codger such as myself still can't believe is what it's become. Back in the day, I wouldn't even think of walking down Alberta without a bottle of Galliano for protection.

Lance also keeps one of the more off-the-cuff booze blogs out there, My Life On The Rocks—a blog unique both for the fact that Lance claims not to edit or think better of anything he writes before publishing, and also for its inclusion of his mistakes and failures. Lance has this wild, anarchist idea that people learn from their failures as much or more than from their successes. Someone, please tuck this guy away on Portland's East Side before his revolutionary notions cause a fire!

When not blogging, opening bars, or inventing fictional bartenders, Lance helped launch the Oregon Bartenders Guild, an organization that has accelerated the cocktail explosion in Oregon, brought the bartender community together, staged events garnering national attention, helped to inspire the inception of the Washington State Bartenders Guild, and most importantly created opportunities for me to indulge in tasty beverages.

I praise Lance for all the formers, and thank him for the latter.

## Milo #2 Cocktail

½ oz. sherry vinegar

4 oz. Bombay Sapphire gin

Orange twist, for garnish

- Pour the vinegar over ice in a mixing glass and shake halfheartedly.
- Drain the vinegar off the ice.
- Add the gin and stir, stir, stir.
- Strain into a cocktail glass.
- Garnish with the orange twist.

## The Swafford

1 oz. Rittenhouse 100-proof rye

1 oz. Laird's applejack

½ oz. Maraska maraschino liqueur

½ oz. green Chartreuse

2 dashes orange bitters

Orange twist, for garnish

- Stir all the ingredients with ice.
- Strain into a cocktail glass.
- Garnish with the orange twist.

*Notes:*

*Maraska is quite a bit drier than the Luxardo maraschino liqueur.*

Milo #2 Cocktail

Portland

## The Lazy Boy

2½ oz. Bulleit bourbon

1 oz. Fig Puree*

1 tsp. 1:2 Honey Syrup*

½ tsp. Ginger Juice*

Lemon twist, for garnish

↪ Shake all the ingredients over ice.

↪ Strain into a cocktail glass.

↪ Garnish with a lemon twist.

## Maestro's Apprentice

1 tbsp. Sambuca Romana

4 coffee beans (preferably a very dark roast)

2½ oz. Martin Miller's gin

¾ oz. Cointreau

↪ Place the Sambuca and coffee beans into a cocktail glass and flame.

↪ Shake the gin and Cointreau over ice.

↪ Strain into the prepared cocktail glass while the Sambuca is still burning.

Notes:

Chris adds a word of caution: *"Although this is a great cocktail for impressing those of us who are more easily amused you must take care not to let the cocktail glass get too hot. If it does, your attempt at being the David Copperfield of cocktails will end in people just pointing and laughing as your cocktail glass shatters. Put simply, scorching hot cocktail glasses and ice-cold cocktails don't mix. The more fragile of the two loses."*

The Lazy Boy

# CHRIS CHURILLA

Chris is the son of a preacher man, so let the man preach...

*"Being the son of a Baptist minister, I did what any good preacher's kid would do and did everything my parents told me not to do. I've always gravitated towards the ideologies of Elijah Craig and Martin Luther King Jr. rather than Billy Graham and Jerry Falwell. However, my father is also an artist who helped me develop a creative side. In 2001, while flailing my way through college, I got my first restaurant industry job working in the kitchen. Those experiences, and a degree in Fine Arts, are to what I owe much of my success. While developing artistically I also developed an appreciation of the culinary arts and learned how to apply my creative inspiration in that way."*

Five years later he found himself bar manager at Downward Dog and Cloud 9 Restaurant, where he is given free reign to come up with whatever weirdness he wants to inflict upon the unsuspecting populace. Chris points out that the lack of a wide variety of bottled ingredients in Corvallis has actually stimulated his creativity. They don't have exotic liqueurs, but they do have figs, fresh botanicals, ginger, and those ever-elusive coffee beans. What more could a minister's son from Salem need in order to make tasty beverages?

The likely highlight of Chris's bartending career has to be the time he met the Munat Bros. at the Great American Distiller's Festival in Portland, where he had taken third place in the cocktail competition. While there was no prearranged prize for third place, the Munat Bros., in a typically crude and self-promoting manner, announced that Chris would be awarded whatever money we had in our pockets. The amount (with assistance from Andrew Friedman) came to $77.77. We had to rummage for food in the dumpsters behind the Teardrop Lounge and hitchhike back to Seattle, but it was all worth it to see Chris's happy little face when we presented him with the pile of crumpled bills, loose change, and lint that we had placed in a paper cup. And for the record, it was all Charles's idea, and he ended up asking if Chris accepted any major credit cards because he had no cash.

By the way, Chris, Charles told me to tell you he'd really like his credit card back.

# KINN EDWARDS

OK, I'm going to come clean here. I don't know much about Kinn Edwards. But what I know I'll share. Kinn has been tending bar for going on about 20 years now in Corvallis, Oregon, and living there even longer than that. Corvallis is a town about 80 miles south of Portland, and home to Oregon State University. The football stadium at Oregon State University is called Reser Stadium. Reser is the company that makes those really crappy cheese dips and stuff that they sell in Qwik-E-Marts for people who are too stoned to walk all the way to the grocery store to get Tostitos.

OK, I agree, the relevance of the last point is questionable at best.

When asking Portland bartenders who should be in an epic and life-altering cocktail book such as Left Coast Libations, the name Kinn Edwards comes up frequently. It is certainly a testament to his skills that this could be the case, considering his remote outpost, as well as his unassuming attitude. When asked about himself, Kinn simply said he is just a bartender doing his best to make good, well balanced, interesting drinks in a timely manner, provide friendly and knowledgeable service, and keep the wine, beer, and cocktail menus interesting and relevant... Boooooooorrrrriinnnnggg!

Kinn's favorite color is blue. He says he likes to write run-on sentences...you and me both Kinn! Kinn and I were both born on the Irish/Pagan/Witch's New Year, November 1st. This must have something to do with it.

Kinn is the man to see at Aqua, a Pacific Rim/Hawaiian restaurant and bar in Corvallis. In keeping with the tropical theme, Kinn features a Trader Vic Classic Mai Tai, a Don the Beachcomber Zombie à la 1934, and The Dark and Stormy. Or you can try one of his own creations using house infusions of green tea, rooibos, or hibiscus, to name just a few. Kinn also fleshes out the menu with a full variety of classics: Monkey Glands, Sazeracs, French 75's, Hemingway Daiquiris, Blood and Sands...

Ok, I'm going. That's all there is to it. Maybe on November 1st, I'll buy Kinn a birthday drink and he'll buy me one. Then we'll light some black candles, invoke the spirit of the crone, drink some pints, and sing "The Fields of Athenry." Meet us there. You know you want to.

## Aqua Sake

1 oz. Junmai Ginjo–style sake

1 oz. triple sec

1 oz. Hibiscus-Infused Vodka*

½–¾ oz. lime juice (to taste)

Lemon twist, for garnish

⋑ Shake all the ingredients over ice.

⋑ Strain into a cocktail glass.

⋑ Garnish with the lemon twist.

## Black Irish

1 teaspoon Ricard pastis

2 oz. Bushmill's Black Bush Irish whiskey

¾ oz. sweet vermouth

3 dashes Peychaud's bitters

Lemon twist, for garnish

⋑ Shake the pastis over ice in a mixing glass to coat it
then strain out the excess.

⋑ Add all the remaining ingredients.

⋑ Stir and strain into a chilled rocks glass (no ice).

⋑ Garnish with the lemon twist.

*Notes:*

*Kinn prefers Martini and Rossi sweet vermouth for this cocktail.*

Aqua Sake

# JAMES PIERCE

James Pierce holds an interest in fine spirits and cocktails that extends back to before he was old enough to legally know of such things in this country. He used to dabble in the conjuring of cocktails for his fellow teenagers, often with satisfying results. This is quite a deft coup to have pulled off. In my youth, I once attempted to do the same for my fellow teenagers, but they shotgunned the cans of Busch and slugged down the whole half pint of Southern Comfort before I even found my barspoon and julep strainer.

Once James turned 21—the instant he turned 21 actually—he left behind the Little Rascals speakeasy scene and assumed the position of bartender at the Crown Royal Bar, which resides on the 200 level of the Rose Garden, where the NBA's Portland Trail Blazers play. (Side note: top secret Munat brother Ben once catered a birthday party for Arvydas Sabonis, 7'3" 300 pound former Trail Blazer from Lithuania—Arvydas flew a lot of his countrymen over for the event. Now THAT was a party.)

James went on to bartend at Demetri's Greek Restaurant and Touché. Touché is a Mediterranean restaurant in Portland's Pearl District, and has a second story with a full bar and six pool tables. Did I mention there are six pool tables? Plus, there are six pool tables. I could be wrong, but I believe that's almost five more than the rest of the bars mentioned in this book combined. So, brilliant bartenders out there, when you go to open a brilliant bar, please, don't forget the pool tables.

It was at 50 Plates that James really learned to elevate his bartending craft (50 Plates has no pool table). Working with LCL'er Lance Mayhew and the indefatigable Suzanne Allard, among others, he learned about the classic cocktails and was provided with the right environment in which to let his freak flag fly. Perhaps it's the opportunity to serve a cocktail alongside a plate of "Hangover Potato Parfait" or $1.50 "Kern Dogs." Or perhaps it's the UPS-brown outfits, or perhaps it really is the company he was keeping behind the bar. But it was at 50 Plates that James came into his own. He remains there as of this writing, and has indeed ascended to the role of bar manager.

50 Plates, by the way, lies in close proximity to Teardrop Lounge, ten01, and Clyde Common. A trip to Portland and a walk among these haunts is highly recommended. Aside from the drinks, food, and company, making a path to each of these places leads to the creation of a rare yet important geometric figure—the staggered inebrioid. For the love of math, check them all out.

## 1st and Final

1½ oz. Bombay Sapphire gin

1 oz. grapefruit juice

½ oz. Maraska maraschino liqueur

¼ oz. Simple Syrup*

¼ oz. lemon juice

2 dashes orange bitters

Lemon peel disc, for garnish

- Shake all the ingredients over ice.
- Double-strain into a cocktail glass.
- Squeeze the lemon peel disc to express the oils over the cocktail and drop in for a garnish.

Notes:

*James says you must use Maraska maraschino liqueur, which is quite a bit drier than the Luxardo, for this cocktail.*

## Winter Hill

2 satsuma wedges

2 lemon wedges

2 oz. Buffalo Trace bourbon

½ oz. Cointreau

2 dashes chocolate bitters

Lemon wheel, studded with four cloves, for garnish

- Muddle the satsuma and lemon wedges in a mixing glass.
- Add all the remaining ingredients and fill with ice.
- Shake well.
- Strain into a Spanish coffee bulb or Irish coffee glass.
- Top with hot water.
- Garnish with the clove-studded lemon wheel.

Notes:

*There are currently two chocolate bitters you can purchase: Aztec Chocolate bitters by Fee Brothers and Bittermen's Xocolatl Molé bitters by The Bitter Truth in Germany. The latter are a superior product but are harder to obtain and much more expensive. You might also look into finding some Scrappy's chocolate bitters, which are handmade in small batches in Seattle, Washington.*

1st and Final

AKA Burro Punsch

## Ephemeral

1½ oz. Ransom Old Tom gin

¾ oz. Dolin blanc vermouth

1 tsp. St. Germain elderflower liqueur

2 dashes The Bitter Truth celery bitters

Grapefruit twist, for garnish

☞ Stir all the ingredients with ice.

☞ Strain into a cocktail glass.

☞ Garnish with the grapefruit twist.

Notes:

*Unfortunately, the Ransom Old Tom gin is so unique in flavor that there is no substitute for it. It's gotten some distribution outside of the Portland, Oregon area where it is made. You may also have luck contacting the distillery directly and ordering it from them. Alternatively, Paul Clarke has published a recipe for an earlier incarnation of this cocktail on his blog (The Cocktail Chronicles), which uses the much easier to find Hayman's Old Tom gin.*

## AKA Burro Punsch

1½ oz. El Tesoro reposado tequila

½ oz. Carpano Antica Formula vermouth

½ oz. Ramazotti amaro

¼ oz. Batavia Arrack

Reed's ginger beer

3 orange slices, for garnish

☞ Stir all the ingredients except the ginger beer with freshly cracked ice.

☞ Add about ½ ounce of ginger beer and stir lightly to integrate.

☞ Put a large cube of ice into a double Old Fashioned glass and arrange the orange slices between the ice & the sides of the glass.

☞ Strain the cocktail into the prepared glass.

Notes:

Dave says the following about this cocktail: *"El Tesoro is the star with its lush fruit, pepper, and smoke. The Carpano and Arrack round the edges with their earthy sweet and spiced notes. The Ramazotti brings a snappy complexity with flavors of toffee, bitter orange, and gentian. Finally, the ginger beer adds a subtle heat and effervescence that ties it all together."*

# DAVID SHENAUT

David Shenaut, bartender magique at Teardrop Lounge, is without any doubt the most wholesome member of the Left Coast Libations glee club. This statement is based upon the fact that he is the devoted husband of a school teacher and proud daddy of one boy and one girl. Come to think of it, Ted Charak, up until recently an integral part of Teardrop, is also married with children. Therefore, I put it to you, dear reader, that Teardrop Lounge in Portland is the most wholesome bar in America.

Oh, but wait. There's still the matter of that Shoemaker guy. Well, there goes that idea. Besides, I'm a dad and everyone knows what a lowlife I am. I guess the jury's still out on Teardrop after all.

Dave has been part of Teardrop Lounge since it opened in July 2007. Prior to that, he worked at Roots Restaurant and Bar in Vancouver, Washington, a town located just on the other side of the Columbia River from Portland. At Roots, Dave enjoyed the chef-owned establishment's love of fresh, seasonal, and local ingredients, and incorporated these into the bar program. He infused vodkas, made his own syrups, and thought he was pretty darn cool.

Dave credits Christian Krogstad, of House Spirits Distillery in Portland, with opening further dimensions of cocktail la-la land to him by force-feeding him a Pegu Club (the cocktail, I assume, not the cocktail lounge in Soho). After that experience, Dave spent months alternating between stroking his chin and scratching his head...thinking.

Then he got a job at Teardrop Lounge. Teardrop has taken those of us in the Pacific Northwest, and sometimes beyond, on a journey to self-actualization. Teardrop has taken the "scratch" bar concept to extents none of us knew. They make everything themselves there. The bar stools? Dave made those. The toilet paper dispensers? Light fixtures? Door stops? Mm-hmm. You know it. And Dave's been there through the whole ride, quietly yet assuredly doing his part to propel Teardrop to its epic heights.

Dave also juggles...and not just his life as bartender, father, and husband. He actually juggles objects. He entertains the kids with it, which is good, because once they've had their juggling fix they can self-entertain for a bit, while Dave hand-knits some bar rags.

# JEFFREY MORGENTHALER

Jeffrey Morgenthaler has been a bartender since 1996, with the majority of these years spent in the quiet little hamlet of Eugene, Oregon. Despite the unlikely locale, he managed to ascend to a position of worldwide notoriety in the bartending world, and this occurred in significant measure due to his blog, the aptly titled Jeffrey Morgenthaler. The blog is read by thousands of people every day, and has been such a success that Jeffrey was asked to speak at the 2008 Bar Convent Berlin—the annual trade show for Germany's bar industry—on how to utilize the web to connect the global bar community. The global bar community has, in fact, become remarkably well-connected in the past few years, leading to increased camaraderie, as well as an increase in bartenders learning from one another, which in turn benefits the lucky, thirsty little consumers such as me. Jeffrey has been a major contributor in bringing this phenomenon about. He says, "You're welcome." And if in the process he just, oh, happens to get his own name out there a wee bit, well...sue him.

It makes perfect sense that Jeffrey would value the power of the web to communicate. It was a little web-based beacon—in the form of the legendary Paul Harrington's articles on cocktails for the online magazine *Hotwired*—that reached Jeffrey in Eugene years ago and really got his excitement flowing for craft cocktails. Today Jeffrey uses the web to share practical information with any bartender, anywhere in the world, who is willing to listen on topics from how to make your own tonic water or ginger beer, to how to make a proper Sazerac, to how to be the coolest guy at the party. (You bring a gallon jug of tasty margaritas...duh.) He then keeps his readers engaged by diligently communicating back-and-forth with them in the comments section. It's pretty stunning actually. There are comment threads over 100 messages long, and Jeffrey is right in there, patiently answering every last question, no matter how inane. That young man is going to make a great daddy some day.

When not blogging, Jeffrey supports the Oregon Bartenders Guild, a group he helped to found. He is also the driving force behind repealday.org, a web site devoted to educating Americans about Prohibition—and why it's good that it ended 75 years ago.

Did I mention he tends bar? He finally moved up the road from his beloved Eugene, and these days is bar manager at Clyde Common in Portland. Clyde has great food and cocktails, and is adjoined by Stumptown Coffee Roasters in the lobby of the always fun and funky Ace Hotel. In the event of World War III, I intend to race to this spot to live out my last eroding days in style. Jeffrey Morgenthaler is, indeed, my choice for the bartender I'd want making me drinks during the apocalypse. He'd make great drinks, keep the mood light, and fight off the wandering hordes of cannibals. That's what being a full service bartender is all about, friends.

## Autumn Leaves

¾ oz. Wild Turkey 101 proof rye

¾ oz. Clear Creek apple brandy

¾ oz. Carpano Antica Formula vermouth

¼ oz. Strega

2 dashes Cinnamon Tincture*

A large strip of orange peel, for garnish

↪ Stir all the ingredients with cracked ice.

↪ Strain into an ice-filled Old Fashioned glass.

↪ Garnish with the orange peel.

## Richmond Gimlet

2 oz. Tanqueray No. 10 gin

1 oz. lime juice

1 oz. Simple Syrup*

2 sprigs mint

↪ Shake all the ingredients well with cracked ice.

↪ Strain into a chilled cocktail glass.

*Notes:*

*You want to shake this drink hard enough so that the mint is chopped up by the ice into little bits, resulting in little green flecks in the glass. If you don't have really hard angular ice, like KOLD-DRAFT cubes, then you may need to cheat a bit and chop some of the mint before putting it in the shaker.*

Autumn Leaves

SEATTLE, for the past few decades, has wielded cultural influence that is disproportionate to its size. This is made all the more impressive given its remote location in *South Alaska*. But from music to television sitcoms to cutesy romantic films to computers to serial killers, Seattle is on the national radar more than one might expect from looking at census bureau numbers.

And world, because we have given so disproportionately to you, we have two simple demands: 1) Bring Kurt Cobain back to life. 2) Bring back our Sonics.

And since Seattle's overall cultural impact has been so disproportionate, it's only logical that its impact on the Cocktail Culture should be as well. And make no mistake: Seattle is a cocktail destination. This is aided, and in some ways fostered, by the presence of brilliant cocktail minds such as Robert Hess and Paul Clarke. But it has flourished because of the legions of amazing bartenders whose numbers grow by the day.

Now here's a surprise: we have some of these bartenders for you! Turn the page and there they will be! Oh my god you are going to love this!

# SEATTLE

Vessel

# KEITH WALDBAUER

Once upon a time, Keith Waldbauer was on a spiritual retreat with Allen Ginsberg in the Colorado Rockies, chanting around the campfire, when a disturbed and hungry black bear emerged out of the darkness and cornered the legendary Beat poet. As others on the retreat retreated, Keith calmly plucked some wild herbs and berries, withdrew a canteen filled with fine bourbon from his hip pocket, and mixed the bear a tasty cocktail. Satisfied, touched, and a little buzzed, the bear gave Mr. Ginsberg a friendly lick on the cheek and sauntered off into the night. His life spared by Keith's calm demeanor and bartending panache, Ginsberg went on to publish his final volume of poems, *Cosmopolitan Greetings*. And the literary world is better for it.

While the preceding story may be a work of fiction, it is the case that Keith is likely the only contributor to this book to have hung out with Ginsberg, and it kind of makes sense that he would have. He's got that sort of Beat-tender thing going on. Keith has been bartending for years, but really emerged into the limelight during his three-year stint at Union in Seattle. Last year, he moved on from Union to help open Barrio, along with fellow LCL'er Casey Robison. And most recently Keith has stepped in alongside Jim Romdall at Vessel. Keith and Vessel constitute a pairing that bears such sublime potential it has many folks all atwitter. And if we weren't all bunged up enough, Keith now also works for Andrew Friedman at Liberty.

Keith is also a cocktail consultant for Kathy Casey Food Studios (Keith apparently likes to work with people who have a "Casey" in their name somewhere), where he designs cocktails for restaurant and bar menus around the country. He writes about cocktails at his own blog, moving at the speed of life, and contributes to Slashfood's "Raising the Bar." Oh, and he's vice president of the Washington State Bartenders Guild. And he's an astronaut, and a professional boxer, and he's in the Friar's Club, and...

OK, that got away from me a little at the end there. But suffice it to say, Keith does a lot of things. Most notably, he makes beautiful cocktails. Keith is one of a handful of bartenders who is able to make drinks that just seem to float. He makes drinks that prompt even the chattiest of people to interrupt themselves upon first sip, and exclaim something along the lines of, "Goddamn that's a good drink! What's in that?"

Or at least that's what I do when I have a Keith Waldbauer drink. Go see him, and see if you don't do the same.

## The Swami

2 oz. Pisco Capel

½ oz. lime juice

½ oz. green Chartreuse

Splash of Simple Syrup*

1 dash Fee Brothers grapefruit bitters

꘍ Shake all the ingredients over ice.

꘍ Strain into a cocktail glass.

*Notes:*

*I think one may need to taste this cocktail and, depending on the
tartness of the lime, adjust the amount of simple syrup used.*

## The Union

4 mint leaves

2 drops rosewater

2 barspoons crème de cassis

2 oz. Hendrick's gin

1 oz. prosecco

1 rose petal, for garnish

꘍ Muddle the mint, rosewater, and cassis in a mixing glass.

꘍ Add the gin, fill with ice, and stir.

꘍ Strain into a cocktail glass.

꘍ Top with the prosecco.

꘍ Garnish with the rose petal.

The Union

## Jasmine Rum Sour

1½ oz. spiced rum

1 oz. John D. Taylor's Velvet Falernum

½ oz. lime juice

¼ oz. Jasmine Syrup*

1 egg white

Angostura bitters, for garnish

- Shake ingredients over ice.
- Strain into a cocktail glass.
- Garnish with a dash of the Angostura bitters on the froth.

Notes:

*Falernum is a spiced syrup from Barbados. You can either purchase this ready-made by John D. Taylor or locate one of several recipes published on the web and make it yourself. Andrew apparently has been using Paul Clarke's Falernum #8 recipe to which he then adds two fresh Thai chilies, which have been split lengthwise. He chooses to just leave them in the bottle, which results in the contents becoming spicier and spicier over time. You may also remove them after one week if you don't want that effect.*

*The froth on this drink must be really thick or the bitters will disperse it, leaving an unsightly hole in your cocktail. See the appendix on homemade ingredients for tips on frothing egg whites. You must become the master of egg whites before attempting this one.*

## Ueno San

1½ oz. Wild Turkey 101-proof bourbon

1 oz. Lillet Blanc

½ oz. Carpano Antica sweet vermouth

4 dashes Fee Brothers peach bitters

A wide strip of orange peel, for garnish

- Stir the ingredients over ice.
- Strain into a cocktail glass.
- Garnish with the orange peel.

Notes:

*Andrew tells us this cocktail is named for the master Japanese bartender Hidetsugu Ueno, famous for, among other things, carving ice balls. Naturally, Andrew builds this drink over a hand-carved ice ball. (He says: "I do this to show off.") Andrew also peels an entire orange in a long strip and winds it around the inside of the glass, à la Crusta, for a garnish.*

*Mere mortals, unable to carve their own ice balls, can still show off by purchasing these from a new venture called Glace Luxury Ice Co. Check them out at www.glace-ice.com.*

# ANDREW BOHRER

In putting this book together, I asked all the contributors to send me a résumé, or bio, or list of accomplishments, or essays titled "Why I'm a Bad-ass," so I'd have some nuts and bolts to work with in constructing a profile for each. A few got carried away and tried to craft their own prose, a serious affront to my precious megalomania.

However, in the case of Andrew Bohrer, even someone as profoundly egotistical as I can recognize that the best recourse is to step aside and let the man speak for himself. Take it away, Mr. Bohrer...

*"Andrew's father told him to be a playboy photographer and a jazz musician (day job, night job). At the age of four, Andrew trusted his father's aspirations to be a mandate—he remains an avid heterosexual, an acceptable photographer, and a champion of the smoking jacket.*

*"Andrew would hate to believe that drinking and serving whisk(e)y (and whisk(e)y's friends) eclipsed playing trombone, but this is somewhat true. Now, he just forces people to listen to J.J. Johnson while he crafts classic drinks and builds tomorrow's. His father deals with it.*

*"Andrew Bohrer dipsographs at caskstrength.wordpress.com, manages the bar Naga in Bellevue, Washington, and is one of the many founding members of the Washington State Bartenders Guild."*

And that pretty much says it all.

OK so let me add a little more. If you are you, which you are, and especially if you are a bartender, which you may or may not be, you must read Cask Strength. From detailed lists of what a pro barkeep keeps in his or her pockets during a shift, to what type of boots best hold doors shut when being rushed by belligerent drunks, to how to balance monogamy with bartending, to how and when to tell a marketing company to go fuck themselves, this is your one-stop resource.

And you should also witness Andrew tend bar. At Naga, from the crystalline pulpit of his own creation, he dispenses liquid egalitarianism like some chanticleer Woody Guthrie. But rather than a guitar claiming to be a machine that destroys fascists, he bears a cocktail shaker inscribed with the proclamation, "These cocktails are the tools with which we will blow up motherfuckers' heads." Look close. It says that.

Update: Andrew's flown the Naga coop and now blows up heads at the brand new Mistral Kitchen in Seattle, where they say they're going to let him put irons in their tandoori oven to make old style flips. Welcome back to the Left Side of the Lake, Mr. Bohrer.

# CASEY ROBISON

Casey works a shift behind the bar as if he's churning out a 12-hour guitar solo for a speed metal band; it's a flurry of activity and intensity that leaves absolute destruction in its wake. It also produces lovely cocktails, which is where the speed metal guitar solo analogy kind of breaks down. But as the saying goes, "who needs analogies when you have cocktails?"

And as Casey reads this, he is undoubtedly sighing and wishing he could recall what it was like to only work 12 hours in a shift. You see, Casey has taken on bar manager-ship at Barrio on Seattle's Capitol Hill, and in a related story, has not seen the light of day in several months. Barrio is a large-scale operation, with an enormous bar, shaped not unlike an amoeba. And it is from this surrealistic pulpit that Casey rocks it...hour after hour, as if Jerry Thomas and the Tasmanian Devil spawned a love child.

Seriously, if you're not on your way to Barrio right now, I just don't know what else to tell you.

Casey honed his chops at several shot-and-a-beer joints around Seattle. However, his life changed when he met Murray Stenson of the Zig Zag Café, and Murray expanded his horizons to see the true magic and beauty of bartending and mixology in their highest forms. Now Casey makes half as much money as he used to.

Since that fateful day, Casey has worked at Café Presse, a favorite place for cocktails, Croque Monsieurs, and soccer games. He also laid waste to Can Can—a cabaret that stashes an astonishing selection of liquors beneath the surface of Seattle's legendary Pike Place Market. He was then off to The Saint, a tequila bar on Capitol Hill, before landing at Barrio. He forgives Murray for ruining his life, and the two speak on a regular basis.

## Something Delicious

1 oz. pisco

1 oz. riesling

½ oz. Lillet Blanc

½ oz. lemon juice

½ oz. 2:1 Honey Syrup*

2 dashes Fee Brothers peach bitters

Orange wheel, for garnish

Lime wheel, for garnish

☞ Stir all the ingredients with ice.

☞ Strain into a coupe glass.

☞ Garnish with the orange wheel and lime wheel on top of the cocktail (not on the rim).

## Adios Mi Vida

2 oz. añejo tequila

1 oz. cream sherry

1 oz. Demerara Syrup*

Brandied or amarena cherry, for garnish

☞ Stir all the ingredients with ice.

☞ Strain into a cocktail glass.

☞ Garnish with the cherry.

*Note:*

*Casey says to use the best grade of cream sherry you can find for this cocktail.*

*Make no mistake: This is a dessert cocktail.*

*See the note on cherries in the appendix.*

Adios Mi Vida

# DAVID NELSON

David ranks among Seattle's coolest bartenders, and is definitely the easiest to find. He manages the bar at Spur Gastropub, and now does the same at Tavern Law. And if you need him, those two places are where he'll be...always. If you walk in and don't see him making drinks, wait a few minutes, and he will emerge from some back part of the establishment, carrying pots of steaming hot syrups or jars of tinctures. In the past I entertained notions that he slept at Spur—on a bed underneath the bar. Spur being a spot for molecular gastronomy, they have a special foam that turns into a bed, provides a night's worth of comfortable rest, then disintegrates before opening time the following day.

David does tinker in molecular mixology, forming a somewhat dangerous combination with the chefs, leading to some bizarre creations and the occasional explosion. But I don't think anyone, including David himself, thinks of him as a molecular mixologist. He's more a proponent of classic, craft, from-scratch cocktails. Just as Matisse would leave portions of the canvas blank if he could not account for the brush strokes, David will not cover a drink in elderflower foam unless it's absolutely called for (or if he correctly guesses that it will sell well with the trendy Belltown crowd). But really, I think David is most interested in whatever ensures he will work 120 hours per week.

He's a Cali kid who relocated to Seattle in 2002. Wishing to ensure a future career in bartending or elsewhere in the service industry, he wisely attained a bachelor's degree in philosophy from Seattle University. This worked magnificently, and today one is hard-pressed to find a block in the Belltown neighborhood that doesn't house a former slinging spot of David's. They include Campagne, Union, Tavolata, Sonya, Mistral, and the much beloved and now sadly defunct Marjorie. Along the way, he and Spur have been featured in the *Seattle Weekly*, *Seattle* magazine, *Seattle Times*, and the much beloved and now sadly defunct *Seattle Post Intelligencer*.

Tavern Law is the newest outgrowth of David's partnership with Spur chef/owners Dana Tough and Brian McCracken. The space moves away from the gastropub gestalt of Spur and fully embraces the charm of the Prohibition era and the yesteryear of craft cocktail glory. And as you might imagine, we're all relieved David has finally found something to do with himself during his ample free time.

Foreigner

## Kentucky Tuxedo

2 oz. Bulleit bourbon

½ oz. dry amontillado sherry

½ oz. Lavender Syrup*

2 dashes Regan's orange bitters

Orange peel, for garnish

☙ Stir all the ingredients with ice.

☙ Strain into a chilled cocktail glass.

☙ Garnish with the orange peel.

*Notes:*

*David says this is his variation on the original Tuxedo, which is made with gin.*

## Foreigner

Strega

2 oz. rye

½ oz. Ramazotti amaro

2 dashes orange bitters

2 dashes Fee Brothers peach bitters

Orange peel disc, for garnish

☙ Prepare a cocktail glass by rinsing it with Strega.

☙ Stir the remaining ingredients with ice.

☙ Strain into the prepared cocktail glass.

☙ Flame the orange peel over the cocktail then drop in the peel.

# ROBERT ROWLAND

Of all the gifted artisans in this book, of all the revered smiths of the craft, Robert Rowland is the only one—the only one—to have the common sense (and common decency!) to ply his trade within walking distance of my home. For this alone he deserves a special reward, which he often receives in the form of my company until (or past) closing time.

Robert is bartender supreme at Oliver's Twist, one of my favorite places. Perched upon Phinney Ridge in Seattle, with the Cascade Mountains in one direction and the Olympics in the other, Oliver's has captured the affections of the area's residents. Even late on a weekday night, one can walk past the silent wholesale bread shop and darkened church across the street, stride on by the closed wash-your-own-dog place next door, before entering Oliver's to a stunning cacophony of mostly very beautiful people enjoying excellent (and enormous) cocktails and nibbling on delicious little bites of food. It is at this moment that one thinks, "Ah crap. No seats at the bar. And Robert's too busy to hang out and chat with me. I'm going home."

That, friends, is the sign of a good bar.

The story of how Robert came to work at Oliver's is a unique one. He actually was working as a bartender at a place that shan't be named—but suffice to say was a high volume, drone-like establishment—when he was enlisted to install the stereo system at Oliver's Twist. Months later, when an opening for a bartender materialized, he was brought on. While the bar program at Oliver's was more ambitious and evolved than what Robert had done previously, he quickly embraced it, and has since carried it to loftier heights than had previously been realized. He educated himself in both bartending technique and spirit knowledge through trial and error behind the bar, through research, through chatting the ears off of other bartenders, and through Seattle's favorite pastime: sitting at Murray Stenson's bar and watching everything he does. Robert even took notes. And he's such a charming and fine-looking young man, I didn't even make fun of him for this...or at least, not as much as I could have.

Robert is fully dedicated, and there's really no telling how far he might take this bartending nonsense before all is said and done. He definitely takes it all very seriously. I was there one night when he asked fellow LCL'er Anu Apte what her favorite Violette was. When she responded with an answer that differed from his own preference (G. Miclo), he informed her they could no longer be friends.

He was only kidding. But you know, come to think of it, things really haven't been the same between those two since. Just one more downbeat tale of woe in the heartbreak carousel that is the world of bartenders, folks.

## Bobby Roux

2 oz. blended scotch

½ oz. Elisir M.P. Roux

½ oz. Cinzano sweet vermouth

½ oz. Cinzano dry vermouth

2 dashes The Bitter Truth aromatic bitters

Lemon twist, for garnish

Notes:

*Robert recommends using Johnny Walker Black for this cocktail.*

꙾ Stir all the ingredients with ice.

꙾ Strain into a cocktail glass.

꙾ Garnish with the lemon twist.

## St. Magnus

8 mint leaves

2 slices Meyer lemon

1½ oz. Herradura blanco tequila

½ oz. Ginger Juice*

½ oz. 1:1 Agave Nectar Syrup*

¼ oz. lemon juice

¼ oz. Aperol

Ginger beer

Notes:

*Robert says in place of the ginger juice you may try muddling three quarter-sized discs of fresh ginger in the glass. Do this before muddling the mint and lemon, which should not be pressed as hard as the ginger.*

꙾ Very gently muddle the mint and Meyer lemon slices in the bottom of a double rocks glass.

꙾ Fill the glass with ice.

꙾ Add all the remaining ingredients except for the ginger beer.

꙾ Stir and top with ginger beer.

St. Magnus

## Navaran

1½ oz. London dry gin

1 oz. Patxaran

1 oz. pink grapefruit juice

¼ oz. lemon juice

1 tsp. Simple Syrup*

½ cardamom pod, grated

1 whole cardamom pod, for garnish

Lemon twist, for garnish

- Shake all the ingredients over ice.
- Double-strain into a cocktail glass.
- Garnish with the whole cardamom pod and lemon twist.

*Notes:*

*Patxaran (pronounced "pacha-RAN") is a sloe-flavored liqueur from Spain. Additional flavorings include anise, coffee beans, and vanilla.*

*Jay says you can substitute Dubonnet rouge for the Patxaran, albeit to different effect.*

*See "Cardamom" in the appendix on homemade ingredients for a discussion on how to incorporate the cardamom into this cocktail.*

## Cavale

1½ oz. Busnel calvados

½ oz. Pineau des Charentes rouge

½ oz. St. Germain elderflower liqueur

½ oz. lemon juice

Dry Normandy cidre de pomme

Wide lemon peel, for garnish

- Shake all the ingredients (except cider) over ice.
- Double-strain into a cocktail glass.
- Top with cider.
- Garnish with the lemon peel.

*Notes:*

*Pineau des Charentes is a regional aperitif from western France made from unfermented grape juice and cognac. The rouge version called for in this cocktail is a little less common and a little harder to find than the regular blanc.*

*Jay prefers the Etienne Dupont brand of cider for this cocktail.*

# JAY KUEHNER

I stand before you, dear reader, intimidated by the task of describing Jay Kuehner. Let's see...amazing bartender, landscape artist, film reviewer, long distance runner, works out of a closet-sized bar, prefers to wear his shirts unbuttoned...

Forget it. There's no real way to bring it all together into anything cohesive.

For as long as I've known Jay, he's been tending bar at Sambar, a tiny space on the backside of the seminal Seattle French restaurant Le Gourmand. From the aforementioned closet-sized bar, Jay spins spectacular drinks and equally impressive conversation, all the while surrounding himself with mounds of rare spirits, elegant little carafes of fresh juices, and water-filled glasses housing all varieties of herbs plucked in the yard. Standing chest to chest with fellow imbibers in the often-crowded Sambar, one might spot Jay, slightly hunched and muttering, pressing through the crowd to get outside, hoping to pick more from the garden or haul a case of something-or-other from the little house out back. There's really no other place like it.

No one in the world, at least not anyone I have come across, makes drinks like Jay. And no one should try either. Jay does what Jay does, and you do what you do. That's how it is. But feel free to be inspired. Most people are, including some of the very finest bartenders I know. Jay is like a one-man midlife crisis for bartenders. Many accomplished ones have paid a first visit to Jay, only to come away with an overwhelming feeling that they must now completely re-think and re-evaluate the manner in which they approach their trade. Such is his originality.

The originality of Jay is preserved by the fact that he dwells in his own realms...you know, those film reviewer/long distance runner/landscape artist/bartender realms. It's commonly known as "The Jay Realm." Population = 1. Jay is, in short, one of the bartending world's best-kept secrets. His bar is usually packed with adoring and loyal patrons. But outside that tight circle, he remains a subject of mystery and intrigue. I think he likes it that way. We like him that way, too. So why am I writing about him? I'm ruining everything. I really should just shut the hell up. Forget everything you've read, and forget everything you know about Jay. Please.

# JIM ROMDALL

Jim is bar manager and part owner of Vessel in Seattle, a bar that by all accounts seems to have officially achieved "legendary" status. Telling anyone in the cocktail world that you work at Vessel carries immeasurable clout. I should know. I tell people I work at Vessel all the time. It works.

But Jim, unlike me, actually does work at Vessel. Jim actually works at Vessel more than most people even realize. If you've been to Vessel and been impressed by what you experienced, or if you go some day and it blows your skirt up, keep in mind that Jim is the one who's there all hours of the day and night, working tirelessly to ensure that all the opulence and majesty comes off with aplomb. He is, in essence, the glue that holds it all together.

But don't let his glueness (IS a word!) lead you to believe he can't also sling drinks like a fool. He knows his stuff, handles everything that comes his way without flinching, and comes up with some extraordinary drinks. When Jim was chosen for the Rising Star Chefs' Mixologist Award in 2009, extra enthusiasm went into Seattle bartenders' and cocktailians' collective fist pump. Ecstatic were we to see the man finally get some of the recognition he deserves.

Jim also has two pinball machines. And this is where my beef with Jim comes in. He keeps these machines at his house rather than at Vessel. What's up with that? I want to watch my world-class cocktail sweat onto the glass top of the pinball machine as I thrust my pelvis this way and that, talking dirty to the pinball flippers, making my Apricot Cardamom Flip tilt. Why deny me, and others, such a sensual experience? The Vessel web site greets its guests with "Modern Nightlife, Timeless Style, Landmark Location, Liquid Elegance." Just tack on "Friggin' Pinball Machine!!!" and we're good. Done deal. What more do I need to say to make this happen? Are you with me on this, people?

## El Globo Rojo

1¼ oz. Tequila Por Mi Amante*

½ oz. Ramazzotti amaro

½ oz. Hardy's Whiskers Blake tawny port

1 dash Angostura bitters

&#8766; Stir all the ingredients with ice.

&#8766; Strain into a cocktail glass.

Notes:

*Jim says you can substitute another tawny port for the Hardy's if you cannot find it.*

*The Tequila Por Mi Amante and the tawny port make this a rather sweet cocktail. Be sure that you stir it long enough so that it is appropriately diluted.*

## Apricot Cardamom Flip

1½ oz. Laird's applejack

¾ oz. lemon juice

½ oz. Rothman & Winter Orchard Apricot brandy

¼ oz. 2:1 (AKA rich) Simple Syrup*

1 dash Cardamom Tincture*

1 whole egg

&#8766; Shake all the ingredients like crazy over ice.

&#8766; Strain into a cocktail glass.

Notes:

*Jim did not call for a garnish on this cocktail but I would recommend a dusting of ground cardamom. Grind about 5–10 decorticated cardamom seeds by hand in a mortar and pestle or an electric spice grinder. Put the resulting powder into a tea strainer and tap over the cocktail to dust the top before serving. Regrind what's left behind if you're not getting enough to go through the strainer.*

El Globo Rojo

# ANU APTE

Anu is a serious contender for the title of "World's Greatest Human Being," and it is somewhat of an urgent matter that she become world famous soon. You see, wherever Anu goes and is not recognized, she is chronically underestimated. The only possible remedies to the situation are either radically altering the stereotypes that plague humanity, or vaulting Anu to such levels of superstardom that there is no place on Earth she can go and not be recognized. While the former would affect more holistic change for our earth, the latter seems a little more attainable, and also figures to be a more lucrative deal for Anu. So we'll opt for that one.

Specific to the subject of drinking, Anu likes her cocktails brown, bitter, and spirituous...you know, "man drinks." She is also excited to incorporate some of the flavors of her ancestral India into the realm of classic-style cocktails (see Sour, Saffron Sandalwood). But if you step into her bar she'll merrily make whatever your heart desires, no matter how pink or fruity or "girly," and make it with skill. And she won't even judge you if your tastes aren't as bodacious as hers...at least not outwardly.

Anu started bartending in the always glamorous and beguiling Utah nightclub scene. Upon relocating to Seattle, she alternated periods of bartending with stints as a banquet manager, event planner, and cocktailer, amongst other ventures. She eventually secured a spot as a bartender at Vessel, where she was sometimes greeted by thirsty customers who asked her, "Where is a bartender?" Ah, but they slowly learned the errors of their preconceptions, and realized the unassuming young woman before them was, in fact, THE bartender.

Anu has also been bartending at Rob Roy in the Belltown neighborhood of Seattle, where she quickly developed a devoted clientèle of mostly lonely men, including myself and Murray Stenson. She is a founding member of the Washington State Bartenders Guild and a frequent host and planner of Guild events. She also, along with her partner (some doofus named Zane Harris), co-owns and operates Grain, an event space located in an 1800 square foot artist's loft with a fully operational bar.

Oh, and she and Zane recently became co-owners of Rob Roy, and fully intend to transform it from a very good bar into one of the world's greatest. As of fall 2009, consider Rob Roy one shining bright reason to make a trip to Seattle. There is no doubt it will fast become a destination bar.

Earthlings, brace yourselves for the Anu Revolution.

Saffron Sandalwood Sour

## Saffron Sandalwood Sour

1½ oz. gin

½ oz. lemon juice

½ oz. lime juice

½ oz. Saffron Sharbat*

1 barspoon Angostura bitters

1 egg white

Sandalwood, for garnish
(see note, below)

⌐ Dry shake all the ingredients except for the sandalwood.

⌐ Add ice and shake again.

⌐ Strain into a chilled cocktail glass.

⌐ Garnish with the sandalwood— you can sprinkle powdered sandalwood over the top of the drink, or if you have a stick of fresh sandalwood, grate it over the top as you would with nutmeg.

*Notes:*

*Anu prefers Plymouth gin for this cocktail.*

*A stick of sandalwood is very much harder than nutmeg and I found it very hard to grate. I used sandalwood chips and ground them as best I could in a coffee grinder and then put the result through a fine strainer to lay a "dusting" over the cocktail. I also recommend this over buying sandalwood powder since the wood has very little fragrance in this form.*

## Smallflower

2 oz. reposado tequila

½ oz. Lavender-Infused Honey Syrup*

1 barspoon Laphroaig scotch

1 healthy dash Regan's orange bitters

Orange twist, for garnish

⌐ Stir all the ingredients over ice.

⌐ Strain into a cocktail glass.

⌐ Garnish with the orange twist.

*Notes:*

*Anu prefers Partida reposado for this cocktail.*

## The Sycophant

1 Angostura-Rum Fig Brûlée*

1½ oz. calvados

½ oz. Navan vanilla cognac liqueur

¼ oz. Cynar

Dried Black Mission fig, for garnish

- Brûlée the fig in a mixing glass (see procedure in the appendix), then muddle with all the remaining ingredients.
- Add ice and shake.
- Double-strain into a cocktail glass.
- Slice the dried Black Mission fig about halfway across and slip over the edge of the glass to garnish.

## Charlie's Vacation

1½ oz. gin

½ oz. lemon juice

½ oz. Campari

½ oz. 2:1 (AKA rich) Simple Syrup*

1 egg white

2 drops orange flower water

2 dashes Fee Brothers peach bitters

- Dry shake all the ingredients.
- Add ice and shake again.
- Double-strain into a champagne flute.

# ZANE HARRIS

How far back does Zane's career in the service industry go? Let's put it this way: he was actually conceived and birthed because his parents needed a bar back at one of their restaurants. Rather than hire someone with experience who would need to unlearn bad habits, they decided to simply create a fresh human, and make him into the ultimate beverage-making machine. As Mozart was with the harpsichord, so was Zane with the barspoon and shaker, and at age five he created a cocktail that made the menu at the Ritz Carlton Paris called "The Thundercats Swizzle."

So, I actually made that all up. Shan't we all agree, however, that lies bring us closer to the truth than facts ever will? I certainly hope so, for my own sake.

The truth is that Zane is the child of restaurateurs, and so grew up surrounded by all things culinary. He started bartending at one of his parents' bars; and between intuition, osmosis, and study, he emerged as a master craftsman of cocktails without the benefit of a community of other like-minded bartenders surrounding him. That community took seed when Zane started frequenting the Zig Zag Café and chatting up Murray, Erik, and owners Ben Dougherty and Kacy Fitch. He'd often bump into Jamie Boudreau (then the bar manager at Vessel) at Zig Zag, and if Jamie was by chance not passed out on the bar, they'd exchange thoughts on spirits and cocktails. Wow. Fun, huh?

Jamie eventually hired Zane to join the gang at Vessel. Legend has it that Zane proved his worth his first shift, when he sliced a sizable chunk of his thumb off with a vegetable peeler and didn't faint. That, my friends, is how you establish street cred in this here biz.

Zane's creativity as a bartender, and his gift of making new customers feel at home, ended up having a significant impact on Vessel, and their success as a bar was in no small way a product of his time there. Recently, Zane has moved on to realize his ultimate ambition: the opening of his own bar. He and his better half, Anu Apte, have become co-owners of Rob Roy in Seattle. Zane is now afforded the opportunity to create a bar in his own image...except for all the ridiculous ideas he presents to Anu, before she promptly tells Zane to get a grip on himself.

Trust me. Those two work well together. Rob Roy is going to be something special. And Zane, if you're out there, you're already something special, puddin'.

## Gin Anthem

2 oz. London Dry gin

1 oz. Lillet Blanc

2 drops orange flower water

1 dash Fee Brothers orange bitters

Orange twist, for garnish

꙳ Stir all the ingredients with ice.

꙳ Strain into a cocktail glass.

꙳ Garnish with the orange twist.

Notes:

*Tara says she prefers Pacific Distillery's Voyager gin for this cocktail.*

## Mingo Creek

1½ oz. Old Overholt rye

½ oz. Cynar

½ oz. Carpano Antica Formula vermouth

¼ oz. dry vermouth

1 dash Angostura bitters

Orange peel disc, for garnish

꙳ Stir ingredients with ice.

꙳ Strain into a cocktail glass.

꙳ Flame the orange peel over the cocktail then drop in the peel.

Notes:

*This cocktail was named after the Mingo Creek Association, a group highly regarded as the leading force in the Whiskey Rebellion of 1791, associated with Tom the Tinker. It was our own Ted Munat who suggested it to Tara. (Ted paid me to write this.)*

# TARA MCLAUGHLIN

Tara got her start at Irish pubs in and around Philadelphia. So nothing we Left Coast pansies throw at her is going to faze her in the least. Don't even try. She had to scrap and argue her way just to get a shot behind the bar, and then had to prove she could handle the rowdies and general riff raff.

She could.

She moved to Seattle without a clear plan and managed to land on her feet, taking a cocktailing job at The Hideout, a nifty little spot on Capitol Hill with great cocktails and an even better book of patron- and staff-drawn cartoons. In quick order, Tara moved from cocktailing back to the bar, and went to work.

Fast forward a bit: Tara was offered the opportunity to resurrect the cocktail program at Rob Roy. Once known as Viceroy, and once bearing quality cocktail lounge ambitions, Rob Roy had fallen into the DJ/Jäger/Vodka ñRed Bull zone. And hey, don't knock it till you try it, is all I can say. But that's not what we're here to learn about today.

We're here to learn about what Tara did with Rob Roy. As mentioned in the pages about Anu Apte and Zane Harris, they are now set to make Rob Roy transcendent. But let the record show that it was Tara who first did the heavy lifting to raise this bar out of the mire. Bye-bye went the flavored vodkas and Apple Pucker. In came the nice selection of ryes and scotches and gins. In came a fully realized cocktail menu of Tara's originals and classics intermingled. Cocktailians rejoiced. Shot seekers said, "w'huh?"

Her work at Rob Roy done, her goals there accomplished, Tara now moves on to the next challenge, which will include her go 'round at the auspicious Beverage Alcohol Resource (BAR) week-long intensive training program. She will undoubtedly succeed. She has a love and passion for what she does, and an energy one could even characterize as furious. Her furious energy has left a mark on many other Seattle bartenders. Literally. No, I'm serious. Ask to see their scars.

# ANDREW FRIEDMAN

Andrew Friedman is the ever-so-happy-go-lucky owner of Liberty, a bar where, in Andrew's own words, bourbon is adored and rye is cherished. I once got it mixed up and cherished bourbon and adored rye while I was there, yet again making an ass of myself. Andrew picked me up, dusted me off, and set me back on the right path.

Andrew came to Seattle from Cleveland, way back when in 1991, just in time for the release of Nirvana's "Nevermind," and I'd venture a guess that we don't even want to know what those next several years involved for Andrew. But the era is preserved in part on the walls of Liberty in the form of multitudes of those beautiful hand-made punk show posters, created to fit on a utility pole and one day destined to be appreciated as a modern art form. Liberty is likely the premier gallery of these gems to also offer exceptional cocktails and a ridiculous array of spirits.

Where Andrew Friedman walks it rains bottles of whiskey (or whisky). He has a vast knowledge of the stuff, from what's good, to what's what, to how to get it in the control state of Washington. Andrew works diligently to procure the finest selections for his beloved patrons, and for this reason we often all fixate on Liberty's selection of this and that. But let's not neglect the fact that Andrew is a creator as well as a collector. He is always working on tinctures and infusions and the like, and always incorporating his creations into new cocktails.

And while we're kissing his ass, let's give Andrew some credit in the hospitality realm as well. I once unleashed six cocktail novices upon him on a busy Friday night, and watched as Andrew sat down with them and expertly derived what each of them would like, made recommendations (which were gratefully accepted), and provided drinks that were universally cherished and adored (in that order). It's hard for those of us who know him to fathom, but Andrew really does have people skills. They are employed daily at Liberty and in his role as co-founder and president of the Washington State Bartenders Guild (WSBG).

Liberty is actually almost always packed, so Andrew doesn't really need you to come in. But he wants you to, because he loves you. He told me to tell you that. Well, he didn't, but I know he would have if I'd asked him, which I didn't.

## Bardstown

2 oz. Rittenhouse 100-proof rye

1 oz. Laird's applejack

½ oz. Cointreau

1 dash orange bitters

1 dash Angostura bitters

Long orange twist, for garnish

⌒ Stir all the ingredients with ice.

⌒ Strain into a cocktail glass.

⌒ Garnish with the orange twist.

## Reppiña

2 oz. reposado tequila

1 oz. Lime-Thai Pepper Tincture*

½ oz. pineapple juice

2 dashes of orange bitters

Roasted Pineapple Feather*, for garnish

⌒ Stir all the ingredients in a mixing glass filled with ice.

⌒ Strain into a Collins glass filled with crushed ice.

⌒ Garnish with the roasted pineapple feather.

*Notes:*

*Andrew says he prefers the Angostura orange bitters for this cocktail, which are less "clovey" than other orange bitters.*

*The pineapple juice should be canned 100% unsweetened juice, not from concentrate. This is one of the few times we don't call for fresh juice.*

Reppiña

# ERIK CARLSON

Erik is a Seattle boy. I bet some of the San Francisco people think of him as one of them. But face it, he grew up in Seattle, and now he's back in Seattle. San Francisco; he just used you to get what he needed and then took it back north to us. And we're all gathered around what he brought back, fiendishly cackling as we rub our palms together and get set for a serious hunker-down.

Trash talk aside (sorry about airing the Left Coast's internal dirty laundry here), Erik Carlson did indeed ascend to bartender-topia while on an extended living assignment in the Bay Area. And he has in fact recently returned to the comforts of the Pacific Northwest as bar manager at Moshi Moshi, a delectable spot for sushi and other Japanese cuisine, nestled in the Ballard neighborhood of Seattle.

While on his Bay Area mission, Erik worked alongside fellow LCL'er Duggan McDonnell at the Redwood Room at the Clift Hotel, then went to The Slanted Door, where fellow LCL'ers Erik Adkins and Jennifer Colliau also did dwell, before becoming bar manager at Umami with fellow LCL'er Brooke Arthur. Now, back in Seattle, he works with no fellow LCL'ers. Wow, check out the attitude on this guy. Guess he's decided he's too good for LCL'ers.

When he's not overseeing the bar program at Moshi Moshi, Erik—well, actually he's always overseeing the bar program at Moshi Moshi. In an industry of overworked bartenders, Erik stands out among the most truly beleaguered. But that's how it goes. You know, bourbon doesn't just infuse itself with glazed pecans, nor does rum infuse itself with banana chips. That's just simple scientific fact, as originally postulated by Pasteur. At some point, under cover of night, Erik sneakily revamped the cocktail program at Bricco della Regina Anna, and we're all mighty glad he did.

Erik, incidentally, reports being very happy since moving back to Seattle and highly recommends other brilliant Bay Area bartenders do the same. I'd guess the same applies for LA, Portland, and Vancouver. Think it over. You can crash on my couch until you get your own place.

## Angel's Share

1½ oz. Glazed Pecan–Infused Buffalo Trace bourbon*

¾ oz. lemon juice

½ oz. Navan vanilla cognac liqueur

½ oz. agave nectar

½ oz. egg white

1 organic basil leaf

Orange peel, for garnish

&#9901; Combine all the ingredients in a mixing glass and add ice.

&#9901; Shake vigorously to whip the egg white.

&#9901; Double-strain into chilled 5½-oz. coupe glass.

&#9901; Garnish with the orange peel.

## Spice Trade

1½ oz. Banana Chip–Infused Rhum Barbancourt Réserve Spéciale rum*

¾ oz. lemon juice

½ oz. Averna amaro

½ oz. organic grade B maple syrup

½ oz. egg white

Orange peel shavings, for garnish (see note, below)

&#9901; Combine all the ingredients in a mixing glass and add ice.

&#9901; Shake vigorously to whip the egg white.

&#9901; Double-strain into chilled 5½-oz. coupe glass.

&#9901; Garnish with the orange peel shavings.

*Notes:*

*See general notes on working with egg whites in the appendix on homemade ingredients.*

*To make the orange peel shavings I would recommend using a Microplane 35001 Home Series Coarse Grater (a great tool!) Otherwise the coarse side of an old-fashioned metal grater may be used instead.*

*Barbancourt has recently undergone rebranding and the rum for this cocktail used to be labeled "Barbancourt 5 Star 8-year old." You may still find some bottles with the old label for sale.*

Spice Trade

## Clear Note

1¼ oz. Clear Creek pear brandy

¾ oz. lime juice

½ oz. Briottet Mandarine liqueur

1 dash Simple Syrup*

1 small egg white

↪ Shake all the ingredients over ice.

↪ Strain into a cocktail glass.

*Notes:*

*Erik says if you cannot find the Briottet Mandarine you may substitute the best orange curaçao you can find.*

## Armistice Cocktail

1½ oz. Rittenhouse 100-proof rye

½ oz. Noilly Prat dry vermouth

¼ oz. green Chartreuse

¼ oz. Luxardo maraschino liqueur

2 dashes Fee Brothers Whiskey Barrel-Aged bitters

↪ Stir all the ingredients with ice.

↪ Strain into a cocktail glass.

*Notes:*

*Erik says you must use Luxardo maraschino liqueur— Maraska, which is much drier, is not a good substitute.*

# ERIK HAKKINEN

As difficult as it may be for me, I'm going to momentarily dispense with the sarcasm and sardonic wit upon which I depend, in order to say with all sincerity that it is a joy to be able to herald the talents of Erik Hakkinen in this book. Erik has been a bartender at the Zig Zag Café for several years, and, well, I think many of us already know who his co-worker is. But it cannot be overstated that despite being in the shadow of Murray Stenson, Erik is in his own right a brilliant bartender who treats his customers with utmost congeniality and makes some truly amazing cocktails.

Do something for me. Make the drinks Erik has contributed to this book at home. Then go order the same drink from Erik, and compare. I think there is a very good chance that the drink Erik makes will take on dimensions of delicacy you had not previously experienced. This is an illustration in technique. Erik has that ability to get drinks to their proper chilliness, their perfect dilution. When he nails it, which he often does, the drink seems to ascend in the mouth before falling gracefully, catching itself and levitating for a moment, finally closing the performance with a chassé off stage left...winking as it goes, enticing the imbiber. Time for another taste. Sip, swallow, repeat.

Erik's also really amusing when he's drunk.

Erik hasn't said as much, but I'd venture a guess that he'd describe his approach to cocktail construction as one of keeping it simple. He has an awe-inspiring collection of booze to work with at Zig Zag (which he has helped to build through his own sleuth-work), and a fine palate and knowledge of spirits to match.

One last note about Erik: If Jamie Boudreau is the Cocktail Whisperer, Erik is the Ice Listener. Never have I seen a bartender with such an intense look of concentration while shaking a drink, ear cocked in the direction of the tin. I like to imagine that the ice is slowly, methodically, over the years and years of shaking, revealing all the secrets of life to Erik. The ice is willing to tell us all, but only Erik cares to listen.

Stop in at Zig Zag and see Erik sometime. He's the one standing next to what's-his-name.

# JAMIE BOUDREAU

What can one say about Jamie that he hasn't already said about himself? What effusive compliments could we unfurl upon him that he hasn't already donned? Just as it can be impossible to give gifts to the person who has everything, so too can it be challenging to flatter a master of self-flattery.

We kid because we care.

Jamie is a drink-making savant, a person with a disturbingly profound palate, a force of nature behind a bar, and a walking encyclopedia on the topics of spirits and cocktails. During the period of my indoctrination to the cocktail world, my brother and I would often descend upon Jamie on quiet Sunday nights at Seattle's Vessel, where he was bar manager at the time. We would marvel at both his knowledge and his funny Canadian accent, which we figured he must have been putting on for our amusement, but turned out to be authentic. The education I received sitting on those very expensive bar stools at Vessel played a huge role in making me the cocktail fraud I am today. It was a very pleasurable education, holistic even, as the mind and senses learned in concert.

Jamie eventually moved on from Vessel, spent some time resuscitating some moribund cocktail programs around town, signed on as an ambassador for St. Germain, released his own line of cocktail bitters, and continues to be a prolific and authoritative blogger at spiritsandcocktails.com. Jamie's blog is one of very few filled with enough useful information to make it a worthy place to search for answers to your cocktail conundrums. He shares a number of his own cocktail creations, which are often easy to make at home. He even shares many of his recipes for homemade ingredients, including his now legendary re-creation of Amer Picon.

Jamie has been featured in the media once or twice, and he is always willing to provide this list. It will not fit in this space, but if you ever track him down he carries it with him at all times in a duffel bag slung over his shoulder. The latest outgrowth of his love affair with the media is his own program on Small Screen Network, entitled "Raising the Bar with Jamie Boudreau." This is essential viewing, as you really need to get a load of this guy in living color in order to understand why everyone likes to make fun of him so much—or rather, I mean, in order to fully grasp his brilliance. Yeah.

Jamie's actually been pretty quiet lately. Too quiet. I'm scared, and you should be, too. Few people realize what this man is capable of. He could strike at any time. And when he does, the unsuspecting denizens of Seattle will likely assume that the thunderous roar is merely the Blue Angels warming up for Seafair. None of us will realize that Mount Boudreau is erupting until it's far, far too late. This is our future. I have seen it.

## Starry Night

2 oz. chardonnay

½ oz. Poire Williams (pear eau de vie)

½ oz. maraschino liqueur

Star anise, for garnish

↬ Stir all the ingredients over ice.

↬ Strain into a cocktail glass.

↬ Garnish with the star anise.

## Pax Sax Sarax

2 oz. Glenmorangie single malt scotch

¼ oz. Peychaud's bitters

¼ oz. Cherry Heering

Absinthe

3 brandied cherries, for garnish

↬ Stir all the ingredients, except the absinthe, with ice.

↬ Rinse a cocktail glass with the absinthe.

↬ Strain into the prepared cocktail glass.

↬ Garnish with the brandied cherries on a long pick.

*Notes:*

*Jamie says the cherries "make the cocktail" and are absolutely necessary.*

Starry Night

# MURRAY STENSON

If you've been reading this book thoroughly, you've probably grown tired of hearing about this Murray Stenson character long before reaching his page. So I'll keep this brief.

What does Murray Stenson mean to bartending? Jeffrey Morgenthaler, commenting in his blog after a particularly well-attended cocktail event at Portland's Teardrop Lounge, probably stated it best when he wrote: "If [an] asteroid had landed on the Teardrop Lounge on Saturday, Murray Stenson would have had to teach the entire Pacific Northwest how to tend bar again."

Struggling for words to describe Murray myself, I once resorted to quoting Herman Hesse, who happened to be writing about the Buddha, and of his inward smile, his every finger speaking of peace, imitating and seeking nothing, reflecting quiet and unfading light. That's some heavy stuff to try to deal with while simultaneously drinking a stiff cocktail from Murray's arsenal, but we do what we have to.

Hyperbole aside, the number of bartenders whose passion for their craft was born the moment they first sat at Murray's bar is truly incalculable. His knowledge, his cocktails, his efficiency and precision, and most importantly, the charm and kindness with which he treats every one of his guests, equate to the blueprint on how to raise bartending to an art form.

OK, so maybe hyperbole isn't quite aside yet. But how does one describe Murray without it?

When the day comes that Murray decides to walk away and get some much deserved rest, many a tear will be shed at the Zig Zag Café and across the Pacific Northwest. He is, quite simply, the living embodiment of what a bartender can, and should, mean to a community.

## Stephan's Sour

1½ oz. Beefeater gin

½ oz. lemon juice

½ oz. Simple Syrup*

2 dashes The Bitter Truth celery bitters

↪ Shake all the ingredients over ice.

↪ Strain into a cocktail glass.

## Queena's Arm

1¾ oz. Beefeater gin

½ oz. Elisir M.P. Roux

2 dashes The Bitter Truth Jerry Thomas' Own Decanter bitters

↪ Stir all the ingredients with ice.

↪ Strain into a cocktail glass.

Queena's Arm

VANCOUVER is a beautiful and elegant metropolis where they recognize some simple universal truths we here in the states can't, such as: 19-year-olds are no more likely to be imbeciles when drinking than 21-year-olds; Cuban rum should be served and drunk because it tastes swell; and the metric system is not the spawn of the devil (in fact, metric measurements just might make for cocktails a tad more precise than ones measured in mutchkins or kilderkins, or whatever it is we non-metric types use).

Vancouver also knows how to make amazing cocktails and serves them in spots where you'd most certainly want to have them. We here in Seattle are a little mad at them for sending us Jamie Boudreau, but our Left Coast community is based on forgiveness, love, and imbibables. Vancouver is a trove of all three. The small sampling of Vancouver bartenders here is certainly not indicative of the scope and quality of the Vancouver cocktail scene, which is thriving. Let's just say we're limiting you to a peek at British Columbia in order to preserve its mystique. Head on up, find these boys, and they will shepherd you in the proper direction from there. And there are many proper directions.

Oh, and our bartenders from Vancouver are so nice they gave us their recipes in ounces. They really shouldn't encourage us Imperial system folks.

# VANCOUVER

West

# DAVID WOLOWIDNYK

According to our friend Dänny Ronen, David Wolowidnyk claims to have been a bartender since 1986, and has been a good bartender since 2000. These days, David seems determined to make up for the 14 years of suck he inflicted upon the good people of Vancouver by becoming nothing short of an amazing bartender.

By the way, David looks like he's about 26 years old. And he's been tending bar for 23 years? What the hell is going on up there in Canada? Either he's been slinging drinks since he was three or there's really a lot to be said for the whole universal health care thing.

Once I was on a bus with Dänny Ronen and our beloved photographer Jenn Farrington, headed from San Francisco to Sonoma for a day of revelry and wine tasting. The topic of discussion was David Wolowidnyk. This, folks, is how bartending legends are spread. And while Vancouver may not be the best place to soak up the limelight, it is a very strategic place from which to originate mystery and intrigue.

The man behind the legends, mystery, and intrigue is in actuality a notably modest and humble person. His Passage to India cocktail is a brilliant concoction featuring the highly unlikely ingredient of Orchid Mango liqueur, in an even more unlikely combination with yellow curry powder. Yet when asked about the cocktail, David prefers to talk about how it was Jenn Farrington who inspired the drink (she is pretty inspiring).

Incidentally, David works the bar at West, a five-time-winner of *Vancouver* magazine's Restaurant of the Year. *Vancouver* magazine also recognized David as Bartender of the Year in 2008, as did the Urban Diner Restaurant Awards. David is clearly a bartending marvel, and were it not for my lengthy and startling criminal record, I would surely cross the border on a regular basis to go see him ply his trade.

I did finally get the chance to meet David when he made the journey all the way down to Seattle to pay his respects to Murray Stenson at Murray's birthday party, and he was simply a peach. I thought he kind of overdid it with the kissing of Murray's pinky ring, but hey, who am I to nitpick?

Bergamo

## Bergamo

5 espresso beans, plus one for garnish

1 raw sugar cube

4 blood orange quarters, 1½" thick

1 oz. Appleton Reserve rum

1 oz. Amaro Montenegro

2 dashes Fee Brothers orange bitters

3 oz. orange juice

1 thin half wheel of blood orange, for garnish

- Muddle 5 espresso beans & sugar cube in a mixing glass.
- Add the blood orange quarters and continue muddling.
- Add the remaining ingredients.
- Shake very well over ice.
- Double-strain over fresh ice into a double rocks glass.
- Garnish with the thin half wheel of blood orange and the remaining espresso bean.

*Notes:*

*The blood orange quarters should include the peel, which adds much to the character of this cocktail.*

*Amaro Montenegro is not currently imported into the United States, though that may change by the time this book is published. Either Averna or Ramazotti may be used as a substitute, each to a slightly different effect. I also recommend trying Smith & Cross Jamaican pot still rum instead of the Appleton. At 57% ABV it packs a bit more of a kick and loads of flavor.*

## Passage to India

1 slice fresh jalapeño chili, about the size of a dime

1½ oz. Flor de Caña Aged White 4-year rum

1½ oz. Orchid mango liqueur

¾ oz. lemon juice

¼ oz. Simple Syrup*

⅛ tsp. curry powder (*"aromatic & floral"*)

10 cilantro leaves, plus 1 cilantro leaf for garnish

- Muddle the jalapeño slice in a mixing glass.
- Add all the remaining ingredients and fill the mixing glass with ice.
- Shake vigorously until very chilled.
- Taste and adjust if necessary with sweetness (simple syrup) or acidity (lemon juice).
- Fill a sling or Collins glass ¾ of the way up with crushed ice.
- Double-strain the cocktail into the iced glass.
- Float the single cilantro leaf on the surface.

*Notes:*

*David, who lives in Vancouver, British Columbia, originally called for Havana Añejo Blanco rum for this cocktail which is not available in the United States because it is made in Cuba.*

*As of this writing Orchid liqueurs have only limited distribution in the United States, in a few western states like Washington. I am not sure if there's any substitute for it. You may try to contact the distributor, 888 Imports Inc. in Denver, Colorado, to find out if it is available in your area.*

# JOSH PAPE

Josh Pape seems to be deftly painting a circle with his life. He started in Vancouver, working alongside former Bartender of the Year Mark Brand at Chambar, before victory in a 42 Below Vodka cocktail competition sent him on a journey to New Zealand for World Cups and other such tomfoolery. This trip, in turn, guided Josh to Australia, where he spent a year working at Hemmesphere and Hugo's Bar Pizza, learning from three-time Australian Bartender of the Year Marco Faraone. He then returned to Vancouver and settled back in at Chambar, this time as bar manager.

But this was not the completion of the circle. The tale as told thus far would in itself be one of those extremely cool Zen circles, the one that doesn't quite connect completely, and so leaves possibilities open. But Josh apparently wanted to add an inflection subtly upwards to suggest what those possibilities would entail. And so he is now the proud co-owner of The Diamond, a bar and bistro in the Gastown area of Vancouver, which he shares with fellow bartenders Sophie Tavernier and, yes, the aforementioned Mark Brand. It's said that Josh's travels to the South Pacific wield influence over the drinks and cuisine of The Diamond, and they've even hired an Aussie, Josh's former colleague at Chambar, Charles Ainsbury, to help out behind the bar.

So the circle is wrapped up into a nice tidy little package, which admittedly is not very Zen. Nonetheless, let us reflect upon the Zen wisdom: The way of the wise is to act—but not compete.

Whoops. Josh does compete. And he wins. He won that 42 Below competition, and a Maker's Mark competition, and a trip to France for the Giffard competition; and he won the 2009 *Vancouver* magazine Bartender of the Year award... Let's face it: Josh isn't very Zen. I give up. But who cares? Name me one great Zen bartender. OK, Jerry Thomas once famously wrote, "as soon as the beer ceases to run freely, a vent is placed in the bung," which is a pretty mystical statement, but still not quite Zen.

So please forgive Josh for such totally irrelevant things, and get to Vancouver to enjoy his miraculous beverages and support his fledgling establishment. A bartender-owned bar is a precious, precious thing.

Someday, the world will be filled with them. I have seen this, and it will be true.

## Booker's Vice

2 tbsp. fresh white corn

2 oz. Maker's Mark bourbon

1½ oz. white grape juice

¼ oz. Amaro Montenegro

¼ oz. Buckwheat Honey Syrup*

1 dash egg white

1 dash Regan's orange bitters

Cracked black pepper, for garnish

☙ Muddle the corn in a mixing glass.

☙ Add all the remaining ingredients and ice.

☙ Shake until frothy.

☙ Fine strain into a large coupe glass.

☙ Garnish with the cracked pepper.

*Notes:*

*Josh says that the corn should be cut freshly from the cob for this cocktail.*

*Amaro Montenegro is not currently imported into the United States, though that may change by the time this book is published. Either Averna or Ramazotti may be used as a substitute, each to a slightly different effect.*

## La Fée de Bohème

1½ oz. Broker's gin

1½ oz. apple juice

½ oz. absinthe

4 chunks fresh pineapple

2 basil leaves

1 dash lemon juice

1 dash Simple Syrup*

Pineapple spears, for garnish

Orange zest hay, for garnish (see note below)

☙ Shake all the ingredients over ice until frothy.

☙ Strain into a highball or Collins glass filled with fresh ice.

☙ Garnish with one or more pineapple spears and the orange zest hay.

*Notes:*

*You may want to lightly muddle the pineapple and basil before adding the remaining ingredients if you do not have hard angular ice (KOLD-DRAFT cubes) for shaking.*

*To make the orange zest hay I would recommend using a Microplane 35001 Home Series Coarse Grater (a great tool!). Otherwise the coarse side of an old-fashioned metal grater may be used instead.*

La Fée de Bohème

# APPENDIX: HOMEMADE INGREDIENTS

A hallmark of the current cocktail renaissance is the flourishing of interest in so-called housemade or homemade ingredients. There are several motivations for this interest. In some cases, bartenders wishing to make a pre-Prohibition cocktail have no choice but to research and re-create ingredients no longer in commercial production. In other cases there is an attempt to "rescue" some ingredient from the clutches of artifice (e.g. high-fructose corn syrup, artificial flavor and color) and restore it to its rightful place on the backbar. Finally, modern bartenders, like their counterparts in the kitchen, are experimenting and expanding the spectrum of available flavorings and scents to create entirely new and novel cocktail experiences (which a subsequent generation will no doubt ponder and scramble to recreate themselves). Whatever the reasoning, sipping a cocktail made with a homemade ingredient is always an extra special treat, and the person making it can always take a little extra pride. We encourage you to make these ingredients, take that extra pride, and savor that extra pleasure when sipping.

Recipes for the homemade ingredients have been collected here and listed in alphabetical order. Each recipe also includes a reference to the cocktail that calls for it.

All of these recipes have been tested (some several times) and the steps made as clear as possible, to ensure you'll be successful making them. In some cases you'll also find notes that indicate sources for hard to find items, describe specialized techniques and equipment, or otherwise help you avoid making mistakes.

## MAKING AND USING HOMEMADE INGREDIENTS

**EQUIPMENT:** Most of the homemade ingredient recipes require nothing more than common kitchen equipment (saucepans, measuring cups, funnels, etc). A few others, however, will require more specialized equipment like a whipped cream canister, a silicone baking mat (sold under the brand name Silpat at many cookware stores), an immersion blender, a precision electronic scale, etc. Be sure to read through the recipes carefully to make sure you have everything you need before starting.

**CONTAINERS:** It's best to lay in a good supply of jars and plastic storage bottles if you intend to make, store, and dispense many homemade ingredients. I'd recommend buying Mason jars in the half-pint, pint and quart sizes. Most supermarkets and hardware stores carry these. You will also need plastic squeeze bottles in several sizes. The best places to buy these are at a local restaurant supply store. Reusing the clear plastic containers in which deli items (like olives) are packaged is also a great and "green" option. Dropper bottles, good for storing and dispensing tinctures and bitters, can be purchased at local herb supply stores and on the Internet.

**FILTERING:** Cheesecloth, muslin, and coffee filters can all be used to remove particulate matter from your infusions. Which to use (and in what combination) depends on what it is you need removed. The finer the particle, the more effort it will take to filter out. If you are using coffee filters to catch really fine particles, it may take a very long time to remove them. Be patient. Also be prepared to change papers and/or filter the ingredient in several smaller batches. If you really want to get hot and heavy into this part of the process, you can purchase a Buchner filter and vacuum pump, which both increase the efficiency of filtering and the speed at which it happens. The best and least expensive place to purchase one of these is on eBay. (NOTE: A Buchner filter is not suitable for applications where you want some amount of particulates to remain suspended because they contain flavorings or add desirable texture.)

**STORAGE:** Homemade ingredients without sufficient alcohol and/ or acid in them should be stored in the refrigerator, lest they get moldy or otherwise spoil. A notable exception to this is the Tequila Por Mi Amante. Despite being highly alcoholic, the fruit in this tasty infusion will oxidize over time. Refrigeration is an option, but it's really just best to use up this ingredient quickly by making cocktails.

**SPIRITS FOR TINCTURES:** Tinctures and infusions typically use grain neutral spirits as a starting point because they add no flavor or aroma of their own. For most people this means obtaining Everclear, a brand of neutral spirits made from corn. Everclear is available in two strengths, 150- and 180-proof, though the latter is not sold in all states. The benefit of using a higher proof spirit is that flavors and aromas can be extracted in a shorter period of time. On the other hand, you may need to dilute the resultant tincture before using it. If Everclear is unavailable, then 100-proof vodka may be used as a substitute, though you should probably lengthen the extraction time specified in whatever recipe you are following. Alternatively, you may also try Wray & Nephew overproof rum at 126-proof. However, as this spirit is not completely neutral in flavor, it may not be suitable for all applications.

**WARNING: Everclear and other high-proof spirits are highly flammable and should be handled with care.**

**LOSSAGE:** Refers to the volume of liquid that is lost after an infusion is filtered because it has been absorbed by ingredients like peels, spices, and nuts and cannot be recovered. In most cases the lossage

has been accounted for in the recipe when the notes state how many drinks you can expect to make from a batch of a given ingredient. Your results may of course vary.

**HERBS:** These should be fresh unless otherwise indicated by the recipe. It's worth making special mention that dried lavender flowers (buds) may be used in place of fresh lavender sprigs but are far more pungent. Therefore when substituting you should reduce the quantity of lavender called for by three quarters (or even more).

**HONEY SYRUPS:** Several different cocktails call for varying strengths of honey syrup, from 2:1 to 1:2 (honey to water). I recommend making a 2:1 syrup and then diluting it as required.

**CHERRIES:** Not many drinks in this book call for cherries as a garnish but for the ones that do, it's worth adding a note. I recommend using either a candied Italian cherry called an Amarena (Fabbri and Toschi are the most common brands) or a brandied French-style cherry called a Griottine (several brands are available). Finally, you can also make your own brandied cherries using one of the many recipes available on the Internet. And, while I shouldn't have to say it, I will: commercial maraschino cherries are simply anathema to the entire cocktail movement. They are probably the primary reason so few new cocktails call for cherry garnishes.

The cocktail recipes in this book represent the offerings of top bartenders working at the pinnacle of their craft. Careful editing and proofing of these recipes ensure that if they are followed, you'll be able to recreate the work of these bartenders yourself. Of course, there is also the matter of cocktail-making technique and technology. If you are a professional bartender or an experienced home mixologist, your experiences making cocktails and understanding of ingredients will serve you well. If, however, you are new to this game, you'll find more than a few challenges await you. Here are some pointers to get you started on the right path.

**MEASURING:** For some this is simply second nature but for others not. So let me be explicit: get a set of jiggers and always measure your pours. If you want repeatable cocktails, measure. If you want to avoid always tasting your drinks and adjusting them, measure.

**USE FRESH INGREDIENTS:** There is no substitute for fresh in this business. Squeeze your own juices, snip your own herbs, make your own syrups. Also, keep in mind that vermouth (especially white), sherry, and port (and other forms of wine) will oxidize after being opened. These may be kept, tightly sealed, in the refrigerator to extend their life. Storing in the smallest possible bottles (minimizing air contact) is also helpful. Be ready to dump anything that tastes off. It will hurt, but the people for whom you make cocktails will thank you for it.

**ICE:** If you follow cocktails on the blogosphere you know there is much that is said about ice. There are bars that tout many different types of ice (e.g. cubes, blocks, bars, pellets, crushed, and shaved) and swear by the importance of using the right type for each cocktail. There are bartenders who will take large pieces of ice and crack them into smaller pieces to attain what they consider optimal chilling and dilution of a cocktail. There are bartenders who carve ice balls by hand, more or less to order, for the same reason. And then again, there are plenty of bars (and bartenders) making the most amazing cocktails with the most unremarkable ice imaginable. Science, hyperbole, and aesthetics are all at play when it comes to ice. I'm not going to try to sort through all of it here, but I do want to give you some basics to get you on the right track.

Yes, there is a world of difference between the ice you make at home and the ice made in a really top-end commercial cube machine. Most importantly, ice made at home will be softer and melt faster than top-end cubes (like the ones from a KOLD-DRAFT machine). This has several ramifications for the home bartender: stirred cocktails will dilute faster but chill more slowly with homemade ice; shaken cocktails will get "wetter" and pick up more ice chips with homemade ice (another reason to double-strain); cocktails served on the rocks will get watery faster; egg whites are much harder to properly froth with homemade ice (because the cubes are smaller, softer, and less angular).

*Ice options for the home bartender:*

➣ Get a good set of ice trays, make ice cubes at home, and don't get so lathered up about not having the very best ice with which to work. The old-school plastic trays actually do a pretty good job and other people swear by the new-style silicone molds.

➣ Make small ice blocks at home. There are several techniques for doing this. One is to use rectangular plastic food storage containers or small plastic drink cups as molds. I think one trick is that the mold should be very thin and flexible so that the ice does not shatter when the water expands during freezing. Use a muddler or ice pick to crack the blocks into smaller pieces for shaking and stirring. Ice made like this is also nice for serving in "on the rocks" cocktails.

➣ Buy commercial ice blocks and use an ice pick to hew off chunks as needed. This requires that you have a place to store the blocks. It is also very inefficient since a lot of ice gets wasted in the form of small bits and pieces that cannot be used for anything. (Personally, I think this option is a bit extreme—but I know bars where they do it.)

☞ Make friends with someone who works at a bar with a KOLD-DRAFT machine (or equivalent) and mooch. These machines make tons of lovely hard ice cubes and it may be possible to get some "extra" on days when the bar is closed or business is slow.

Note that commercial bagged ice, like you can buy at the super-market, may not be much better than homemade ice—in fact, it may be worse. The reason for this is that most commercial ice is no longer made in cubes. Instead they use a process that results in lots of small irregular pieces or flat tiles. These are often smaller than homemade ice cubes and melt faster. And since most people put their commercial bag ice in a picnic cooler after getting it home, it can get wet very quickly as it melts.

Another bit of advice: don't get hung up in the whole "making clear ice at home" cult. Even if it's possible, it's not practical, especially when you consider the volume of ice one goes through making a few dozen cocktails.

Finally, a very personal observation: after all the hooha about ice and chilling is over, I find that cocktails served "up" taste better after they've warmed a bit.

**FROTHING EGG WHITES:** Along with the resurgence of pre-Pro-hibition cocktails and cocktail ingredients, we've seen the return of egg whites. When used properly, egg whites can have a dramatic impact on the texture and mouth-feel of a cocktail. They also add a showy, frothy head. The problem, for the home bartender, is that getting egg whites to behave properly can be something of a challenge. And there's something sad (or even gross) about an egg white cocktail that fails to froth.

*Here are some tips and tricks to help you with the egg frothing.*

☞ *Temperature*: Ideally egg whites should be used at room tempera-ture—or just slightly chilled. This is a trick borrowed from baking, where you learn that it's easier to beat egg whites into a meringue when they are not so cold.

↪ *Break 'em Up*: You'll notice that many of the egg white cocktails in this book call for amounts less than a whole egg's worth (see below on this). You'll quickly discover it's hard to measure egg whites unless you have beaten them a little bit before measuring. In fact, if you know you are going to be making a lot of egg white cocktails, it would behoove you to get one of those syrup dispensers with a sliding lid. These are perfect for handling egg whites—the lid "cuts them" when you let go. You can also break them up by shaking after putting them inside the dispenser.

↪ *Don't Over-Ice*: If the shaker is filled with too much ice then there's no room inside for the contents to tumble around and the egg whites won't get properly emulsified and frothed.

↪ *Dry Shaking*: This refers to the technique of attempting to froth egg whites in a shaker before adding ice. Many bartenders swear by this technique and you'll see it specified in a number of cocktail recipes. You'll find, however, that there's a tendency for pressure to build up and for the shaker to separate, sending some of the egg white into the air and onto your hands. If you are using two tins, you should seal them together as tightly as possible, with the little tin at as acute an angle as possible to the large tin. Another technique is to pause and bleed a little pressure off as you go along (i.e. crack the seal by squeezing the tins). You may also find it's possible to hold the shaker together by brute force, but only if you are very strong.

↪ *Shaking with a Spring:* As part of dry shaking, some bartenders will also take the spring off a Hawthorne strainer and put it into the shaker. The idea is that the spring acts like a whisk and helps to whip things up. Sometimes the spring is "balled up" so it rattles around more than if it was just left "long." The spring should be removed before the ice is added.

↪ *Shaking with Hard Ice:* This won't be much help to the home bartender but it will explain how some bartenders get their whites to froth without dry shaking (or any other tricks). If the ice is hard and angular enough (e.g. KOLD-DRAFT cubes) you should have no trouble.

↪ *The BonJour Cafe Latte Frother*: Not everyone can pull off dry shaking, and even with hard ice, it takes some strength to froth whites. Fear not! This handy device from BonJour makes frothing egg whites a snap. You must get a particular model, however—the one with a little wavy steel disc on the end. All the others have a spring on the end, which will not achieve the desired results. The BonJour SKU for this item is 53776.

↪ *Use More*: OK, I admit it: sometimes, when a cocktail recipe calls for only ½ oz. of egg white, I cheat and use a whole egg's worth (albeit from a small egg). It just seems to help if there's more of the white in there to froth up. Note that you are changing the recipe when you do this since the additional egg white will change the flavor of the cocktail.

↪ *Beware of Denaturing and Coagulation:* High-proof spirits, like 100-proof rye, and fruit acids (e.g. lemon juice), can ruin your egg whites. Alcohol will denature (break down) proteins, and acids will cause your whites to coagulate (turn cloudy). Don't use spirits which are more than 90 proof and don't let an unshaken cocktail sit after egg whites have been added to the mixing glass. Add the egg whites last, just before shaking.

**WARNING: Raw eggs may be a health hazard for people with compromised immune systems, the elderly, or women who are pregnant. Use caution when serving cocktails containing whole eggs or egg whites to people who may be at risk.**

## RESOURCES ON THE WEB:

*The Left Coast Libations Web Site (www.leftcoastlibations.com)*

Look here for updates on LCL bartenders, cocktail recipes, and contributions by a growing community of cocktail enthusiasts.

## THE COCKTAIL BLOGOSPHERE

I owe no small debt to the kind souls who have been blogging about cocktails and cocktail culture far, far longer than I have been making cocktails, and who generously share their knowledge and passion with the world. Their writings form an invaluable (and practically inexhaustible) resource for anyone with a keen interest in cocktails. I know my work would not have been possible without them.

A quick survey of the Internet will reveal a plethora of cocktail-related blogs. Here is a short list of my favorites, provided here as a resource to the reader, as well as a small "thank you" for their help and inspiration during the writing of this book:

Alcademics, *Camper English*

Cask Strength, *Andrew Bohrer*

The Cocktail Chronicles, *Paul Clarke*

Kaiser Penguin, *Rick Stutz*

Oh Gosh!, *Jay Hepburn*

A Mountain of Crushed Ice, *Tiare Olsen*

Rowley's Whiskey Forge, *Matthew Rowley*

SLOSHED!, *Marleigh Riggins*

Small Hands Bartender, *Jennifer Colliau*

SpiritsAndCocktails.com, *Jamie Boudreau*

Trader Tiki, *Blair Reynolds*

Underhill-Lounge, *Erik Ellestad*

## AGAVE-GINGER SYRUP

*The Lively, Joseph Brooke*

3 oz. Ginger Juice (see note below)

1½ oz. agave nectar

· Mix the ginger juice and agave nectar together.

· Store in bottle in the fridge.

*Notes:*

*Makes enough for 6 cocktails. It will keep for a couple of months if refrigerated.*

*See "Ginger Juice" in this appendix for procedures on how to make this.*

## AGAVE NECTAR SYRUP (1:1)

*St. Magnus, Robert Rowland*

2 oz. light agave nectar

2 oz. hot water

· Stir together the agave nectar and hot water until thoroughly combined.

· Store in a plastic squeeze bottle.

*Notes:*

*Makes enough for 8 cocktails. It will keep almost indefinitely without refrigeration.*

## ANGOSTURA-RUM FIG BRÛLÉE

*The Sycophant, Zane Harris*

2 oz. Angostura bitters

1 oz. overproof/151-proof rum

1 dried Black Mission fig, halved

· Mix the bitters and the rum in a Misto pump or spray bottle.

· Shake briefly to mix and pressurize the pump, if you are using one.

· Place the fig halves in the bottom of a mixing glass, with the cut sides facing upwards.

· Light a wooden match or lighter and hold it above the glass.

· Spray the bitters and rum mixture through the flame into the mixing glass, keeping the fig lit via short bursts from the pump for 10 seconds.

*Notes:*

*Be careful when handling the mixing glass, as it can get very hot.*

*Use the mixing glass in which the fig was prepared to make this cocktail.*

*Zane recommends using Lemon Hart Demerara 151 or Stroh rum.*

*A Misto pump can be purchased at many kitchen and housewares stores for $10 or less on sale, and is highly recommended. If you are using a spray bottle instead, take care not to drench the fig with the bitters and rum mixture or the drink will come out too bitter.*

## BANANA CHIP–INFUSED RHUM BARBANCOURT RÉSERVE SPÉCIALE RUM

*Spice Trade, Erik Carlson*

½ bottle (375 ml) Rhum Barbancourt Réserve Spéciale rum

¼ lb. dried banana chips

· Combine the rum and the banana chips in a 1-pint jar with a tight-fitting lid.

· Let sit for one week, stirring once or twice a day.

· On the eighth day, strain using cheesecloth and then filter paper.

*Notes:*

*Makes enough for about 9 cocktails. It will keep indefinitely though it may throw a bit of sediment over time.*

*See notes at the beginning of the appendix on straining.*

*Barbancourt has recently rebranded its products. The rum for this cocktail used to be labeled "Barbancourt 5 Star 8-year old" and you may still find (or have) some bottles with the old label.*

*Personally, I feel banana chips (which are dried or fried) don't have a lot of banana flavor. I tried augmenting this recipe by adding a few slices of fresh banana to the infusion and leaving them in until they started to turn dark. You may play with this addition if you like, though Erik did not feel it was necessary.*

## BASIL FOAM

*Fragola e Aceto, Chris Ojeda*

4 oz. Basil Simple Syrup (see next recipe)

5½ oz. egg whites

5½ oz. filtered water

· Combine the basil syrup, egg whites, and filtered water in a 500-ml whipped cream canister.

· Seal the canister and shake to mix the ingredients.

· Charge with one nitrous oxide cartridge and shake.

· Refrigerate for one hour.

· Charge with another cartridge and shake again before using.

Notes:

*Makes enough for at least 10 cocktails.*

*The foam will keep for several days in the refrigerator.*

*Always remember to shake the canister immediately before using it.*

## BASIL SIMPLE SYRUP

4 oz. Simple Syrup (see note below)

Leaves from 4–5 sprigs of basil

· Bring the simple syrup to a low simmer in a small saucepan.

· Add the fresh basil one leaf at a time, removing each leaf from the syrup when it turns brown.

· Taste the syrup as you go along. When the basil flavor is readily apparent, remove any remaining leaves and remove the saucepan from the heat.

· Let cool, transfer to a jar or plastic container and store, covered, in the refrigerator.

Notes:

*Once the simple syrup has been brought to a low simmer, you may turn off the heat.*

*A recipe for simple syrup is provided in this appendix.*

## BUCKWHEAT HONEY SYRUP (1:1)

*Booker's Vice, Josh Pape*

1 oz. buckwheat honey

1 oz. hot water

· Stir together the honey and hot water until thoroughly combined.

· Store in a plastic squeeze bottle.

Notes:

*Makes enough for 8 cocktails.*

*Buckwheat is the most pungent of all monofloral honeys, exhibiting strong molasses and malt flavors. Not everyone likes it and some even find it repulsive. Bamboo honey, made from Japanese knotweed, is similar in character to buckwheat honey, but is less intensely flavored and may be tried as an alternative.*

## CANDIED ORANGE WHEELS

*St. Astor, Christine D'Abrosca*

2 or 3 organic Valencia oranges

8 oz. Simple Syrup (see note below)

· Preheat the oven to 250 degrees F.

· Using a very sharp chef's knife carefully cut the oranges into ⅛ inch thick slices.

· Place the orange slices in a saucepan filled with the simple syrup.

· Bring to a slow boil and steep the orange slices for about one minute.

· Remove the orange slices from the saucepan, using tongs or a slotted spoon, and put them on the bottom of a shallow glass baking dish.

· Pour the simple syrup from the saucepan over the orange slices.

· Allow the orange slices and syrup to cool in the glass baking dish.

· Cover a baking sheet with a silicone baking mat.

· Arrange the orange slices in a single layer on the prepared baking sheet.

· Place the baking sheet in the oven.

· Bake until the orange slices are crispy (see note below), about 45 minutes.Remove the orange slices as they are ready, allowing them to cool on a piece of parchment paper.

· Let the slices firm up completely for several hours, and then store them, loosely wrapped in the parchment, inside a storage container.

Notes:

*Christine's original recipe suggested using a mandoline to slice the oranges but the model to which I had access (and which was not cheap) was entirely unable to cut through the rind and made a mess of the fruit. I am told it may be possible to use a mandoline to slice oranges but it should be one of those very inexpensive models with a V-shaped blade. You can find these for sale at kitchen supply stores like Sur La Table.*

*Check the orange slices frequently while baking them because they are so thin that they can burn easily. I also turned the slices a few times during baking to allow them to dry on both sides. I removed them when the slices were dry on the edges, sometime before they might be considered "crispy."*

*A recipe for simple syrup is provided in this appendix.*

## CARDAMOM

*Navaran, Jay Kuehner*

After a bit of experimentation, here are my recommendations on how to prepare and apply cardamom:

· Use decorticated cardamom seeds instead of pods to avoid having to deal with the husks, which are inedible and tannic.

· About 6 to 8 seeds are the equivalent of a whole pod.

· When using cardamom as a cocktail ingredient, the seeds should be coarsely ground in a mortar and pestle or an electric spice grinder to release more flavor.

· When using cardamom as a garnish, fine grind about one or two teaspoons of the seeds in a mortar and pestle or an electric spice grinder, put the results in a tea strainer and tap to dust the top of the cocktail before serving. Grind the seeds some more if you're not getting enough through the strainer.

## CARDAMOM TINCTURE

*Apricot Cardamom Flip, Jim Romdall*

½ oz. decorticated cardamom seeds

2 oz. Everclear grain alcohol

· Put the cardamom seeds and Everclear in a small jar with a tight-fitting lid.

· Seal and infuse for four to six weeks, shaking once a day.

· Filter through a coffee filter.

· Store in a dropper bottle.

*Notes:*

*The tincture will keep indefinitely. It may be watered down a little if you like, especially if you used 180-proof alcohol.*

## CELERY JUICE

*Southern Exposure, Daniel Hyatt*

Celery juice is most easily made in a centrifugal juicer such as a Champion. However if you don't have access to such an appliance, here are some alternatives:

Blend celery in a small food processor and press the results through a fine-mesh sieve or cheesecloth.

Or muddle some celery in a mixing glass and press the results through a fine-mesh sieve or cheesecloth.

## CHAPULINES

*La Tuna Te Toca, H. Joseph Ehrmann*

These are fried grasshoppers from Oaxaca, where they are eaten as a snack. After being fried they are coated with a little lime juice and sometimes powdered chili as well.

H. recommends muddling 3 or 4 chapulines in a mixing glass before adding the remaining ingredients. The cocktail should be double strained.

*Notes:*

*This ingredient is extremely hard to locate. I tried many sources on the Internet: Nada. If you live in San Francisco, try La Oaxaquena located at 2128 Mission Street, though I was never successful finding them there. Or go to Elixir and pester H. to make one for you.*

*Also note that there's an FDA warning that chapulines may contain lead.*

## CINNAMON TINCTURE

*Autumn Leaves, Jeffrey Morgenthaler*

1 oz. whole cinnamon sticks

4 oz. Everclear grain alcohol

· Put the cinnamon sticks into an 8-ounce jar with a tight-fitting lid.

· Cover with the grain alcohol and let sit for three weeks.

· Strain out the cinnamon sticks.

· Transfer the tincture to a dropper bottle.

## COSTUS ROOT BITTERS

*Sandcastles in the Sky, Daniel Shoemaker*

180 ml. Wild Turkey 101 proof rye

½ oz. costus root (see note below)

½ tbsp. chopped fresh ginger

¼ tsp. dried sweet orange peel

⅛ tsp. fennel seed

¼ tsp. decorticated cardamom seeds

¼ tsp. rose hips

¼ tsp. milk thistle (whole)

¼ bay leaf

· Put the costus root and ginger in a 4-ounce jar with a tight-fitting lid.

· Let sit for seven days.

· Strain to remove the solids.

· Discard the ginger and return the costus root to the jar.

- Add the remaining ingredients.
- Let the tincture sit for two weeks longer.
- Strain out the solids.
- Transfer the finished tincture to a dropper bottle.

Notes:

*Costus root (Saussurea lappa) can most easily be obtained in a Chinese herb store where it will either be called Mu Xiang or by its pharmaceutical name Radix Aucklandiae. When freshly dried, this herb has a woodsy, slightly tangy smell. As it gets old, it will start to smell funky and off-putting. Be sure you are buying fresh root.*

## DEMERARA SYRUP (2:1)

*Adios Mi Vida, Casey Robison*

*The Bull on the Hill, Matty Eggleston*

8 oz. demerara sugar

4 oz. water

- Put the water and sugar in a saucepan.
- Bring the mixture to a boil, stirring frequently.
- Reduce heat to a low simmer and continue stirring until the sugar is dissolved and the syrup is translucent.
- Remove from heat and allow the syrup to cool.
- Transfer to a jar or plastic container and store, covered, in the refrigerator.

Notes:

*This syrup keeps indefinitely.*

*In the United States, demerara sugar is usually called turbinado sugar.*

## DRIED APRICOT–INFUSED PISCO

*Il Terzo, Ryan Fitzgerald*

15 dried sulfured apricots

½ bottle (375 ml) Don César Puro pisco

- Slice the apricots into strips ¼ inch wide.
- Put the sliced apricots in a 16-ounce jar with a tight-fitting lid.
- Cover with the pisco.
- Infuse for three weeks, shaking at least once a day.
- Strain the mixture, pressing the apricots with the back of a spoon to get as much pisco out of them as possible.
- Strain again through a coffee filter to get the clearest possible infusion.
- Store in the same jar in which the infusion was made.

Notes:

*Makes enough for about seven cocktails since the apricots absorb a fair amount of the pisco. It will keep indefinitely, though it may throw a bit of sediment over time.*

*During the infusing process, there's a significant buildup of sulfur dioxide ($SO_2$) in the pisco from all the apricots. In addition to causing problems for those sensitive to sulfites, it adds an off note into an otherwise delicious cocktail. My remedy was to air out the infusion after it was done by leaving the jar open for about 30 minutes. A lot of the excess $SO_2$ "blew off" as it does in white wines that have the same problem.*

## DRIED CHILI–INFUSED ORANGE BITTERS

*The Bull on the Hill, Matty Eggleston*

2½ oz. Regan's orange bitters

1 small dried ancho chili

1 small dried pasilla chili

1 small dried New Mexican chili

· Pour the Regan's orange bitters into a 4-ounce jar with a tight-fitting lid.

· Add all the dried chilies to the bitters.

· Cover the jar and infuse for three days.

· Strain out the chilies.

· Carefully transfer to a dropper bottle or a bottle with a shaker top.

· Mark clearly to avoid accidents.

*Notes:*

*Bulk dried chilies are available for sale at most Latin American groceries and many health-food markets. If you can't find the exact selection of chilies listed in the recipe, feel free to experiment with whatever is available.*

*If the chilies are large you may want break them up a bit so they fit in the jar and are well covered by the bitters.*

## EARL GREY TEA–INFUSED NO. 209 GIN

*English Breakfast, Marco Dionysos*

½ bottle (375 ml) No. 209 gin

2 Earl Grey tea bags

· Pour the gin into a 1-quart jar with a tight-fitting lid.

· Add the Earl Grey tea bags and steep for 30 minutes or less, until the liquid is dark amber but translucent.

· Remove the tea bags and discard.

*Notes:*

*Makes enough for about six cocktails. It keeps indefinitely.*

*I recommend using a fine grade of Earl Grey like that packaged by The Republic of Tea or Twinings.*

## FIG PUREE

*The Lazy Boy, Chris Churilla*

¼ lb. dried Black Mission figs

8 oz. purified water

· Combine the figs and water in a blender and puree.

· Strain the puree through a china hat to remove any large pieces of fig.

· Transfer to a jar or plastic container and store, covered, in the refrigerator.

*Notes:*

*Makes enough for about eight cocktails. It keeps for about a month.*

*I recommend removing the stems and cutting the figs into halves or quarters to make blending easier.*

*A china hat is a conical strainer that comes in a variety of meshes; some are quite fine, like a chinois. Since the seeds will get strained out when the cocktail is made I don't believe you need to use a china hat with a particularly fine mesh.*

*I used water that had been run though a home water filter.*

## FIVE SPICE–INFUSED AGAVE NECTAR

*Laughing Buddha, Duggan McDonnell*

4 oz. water

1 short cinnamon stick

1½ tsp. black peppercorns

¾ tsp. white peppercorns

Half of a star anise pod

1–2 whole cloves

2 heaping tsp. peeled minced ginger

¼ tsp. sea salt

4 oz. agave nectar

· In a small saucepan, bring the water to a boil.

· Add the cinnamon stick, peppercorns, star anise, cloves, and ginger.

· Return to a boil and add the salt.

· Add the agave nectar and bring to a simmer, stirring frequently.

· Remove from the heat and let cool.

· Cover and refrigerate overnight.

· Transfer to a jar or plastic container and store, covered, in the refrigerator.

Notes:

*Makes enough for about 14 cocktails. It keeps up to three weeks in the refrigerator.*

## GINGER JUICE

*The Lazy Boy, Chris Churilla*

*St. Magnus, Robert Rowland*

The best way to obtain ginger juice is with a centrifugal juicer, such as a Champion. Alternatively, you can blend fresh ginger in a small food processor with a little bit of water and then squeeze the result through several thicknesses of cheesecloth. In some markets you can also purchase bottled ginger juice (Ginger People brand), but I have not tried this in a cocktail.

## GLAZED PECAN–INFUSED BUFFALO TRACE BOURBON

*Angel's Share, Erik Carlson*

½ bottle (375 ml) Buffalo Trace bourbon

¼ lb. Frani's Glazed Pecans
  (see next recipe)

· Combine the bourbon and the glazed pecans in a 1-pint jar with a tight-fitting lid.

· Let sit for one week, stirring once or twice a day.

· On the eighth day, fine strain through cheesecloth.

Notes:

*Makes enough for about 5 cocktails (the pecans absorb a fair amount of the bourbon). It keeps indefinitely, though it may throw a bit of sediment over time.*

*See notes at beginning of appendix on fine straining.*

## FRANI'S GLAZED PECANS

2 tbsp. sweet cream butter

2 tbsp. agave nectar

½ tbsp. water

¼ tsp. salt

½ lb. raw pecan halves

· Preheat oven to 250 degrees F and line a baking sheet with parchment paper or a silicone baking mat.

· Combine the butter, agave nectar, water, and salt in a saucepan and bring to a boil.

· Remove from the heat.

· Add the pecans and stir to completely coat the pecans.

· Spread the pecans evenly on the prepared baking sheet.

· Bake until the pecans start to darken, about 10–15 minutes.

· Remove the baking sheet from the oven and allow the pecans to completely cool.

Notes:

*Makes enough for two batches of the infused boubon*

*This recipe was given to Erik by his mom.*

*Keep a close eye on the pecans while baking them because they can burn very quickly.*

*You might want to break up the glazed pecan halves before putting them in the bourbon to expose more surface area.*

## GRAPEFRUIT SYRUP

*The No. 4, Lane Ford*

1 cup organic grapefruit juice

2 cups organic sugar

· Combine all the ingredients in a mixing glass.

· Stir thoroughly with a barspoon until the sugar is dissolved.

· Transfer to a jar or plastic container and store, covered, in the refrigerator.

*Notes:*

*It is important to stir the mixture for a long time, using a mixing glass rather than a bowl. This is a lot of sugar, and what you wind up with after all the stirring may be closer to a suspension than a true syrup (as you would get if the mixture was heated, which you don't want to do for this cocktail). It's possible that after the mixture sits around it may need to be stirred up again to get everything back into the suspension.*

## GRENADINE

*Seven Sins, John Coltharp*

1 liter pomegranate juice

10½ oz. sugar (by weight)

Vodka

· Bring the pomegranate juice to a low boil in a saucepan.

· Boil until the juice is reduced in volume by half.

· Add the sugar and stir to completely dissolve.

· Remove from the heat and allow to cool.

· Add a small amount of vodka to preserve.

· Transfer to a jar or plastic container and store, covered, in the refrigerator.

*Notes:*

*A quick search on the web will reveal there are many recipes for making grenadine. Feel free to experiment. You may also choose to use one of the two acceptable artisanal grenadines now available in some markets: Small Hand Foods (the best in my opinion) and Sonoma Syrup Co.*

*Whatever you do, don't use anything that contains corn syrup. Also note that pomegranate molasses is not an acceptable substitute for pomegranate juice.*

## HIBISCUS-INFUSED VODKA

*Aqua Sake, Kinn Edwards*

½ bottle (375 ml) vodka

½ oz. dried hibiscus flowers

· Combine the vodka and hibiscus in a 1-pint jar with a tight-fitting lid.

· Infuse for four hours at room temp.

· Strain to remove the hibiscus.

*Notes:*

*Makes enough for about 12 drinks. It keeps indefinitely.*

*Dried hibiscus, called Jamaica in Mexico, is available for sale at most Latin American grocery stores and many health-food markets.*

## HONEY SIMPLE SYRUP (2:1)

*The Lazy Boy, Chris Churilla (1:2)*

*Il Terzo, Ryan Fitzgerald ("runny honey" 1:1)*

*Something Delicious, Casey Robison (2:1)*

8 oz. honey

4 oz. hot water

· Stir the honey and hot water until thoroughly combined.

· Store in a plastic squeeze bottle.

*Notes:*

*Many recipes call for honey syrup (or runny honey syrup) at different concentrations, from as low as 1:2 to as high as 2:1 (honey to water). Rather then having to make and keep all these different concentrations laying about, I recommend making one version at the ratio 2:1 and then diluting as necessary.*

## HOUSE CHOCOLATE LIQUOR

*Catch-22, Jackie Patterson*

500 ml Cruzan 151-proof aged rum

1½ oz. Valrhona Venezuelan cacao nibs

½ Tahitian vanilla bean, split length-wise

· Combine all the ingredients in a 1-quart jar with a tight-fitting lid and cover.

· Infuse for three and a half weeks, shaking once or twice a day.

· Pour through a fine-mesh sieve to remove the nibs and vanilla bean.

· Pour through coffee filters in small batches to remove the finer particles.
Replace the filter paper as necessary.

*Notes:*

*It keeps indefinitely.*

*The Valrhona nibs, usually sold in large bags, are available in smaller quantities on Amazon.com. You can also find Scharffen Berger nibs for sale at Whole Foods (which sells them repackaged in half-pint containers) as well as on the Internet.*

*Reminder: you are making a high-proof cacao infusion, not a chocolate liqueur suitable for sipping after dinner.*

## JASMINE SYRUP

*Jasmine Rum Sour, Andrew Bohrer*

Andrew's original recipe called for a brand of syrup made in Thailand called "Hale's Blue Boy." This can be found in better Asian groceries in cities like San Francisco and Vancouver. However, Hale's is artificially flavored and I didn't care for it. I spent some time trying to figure out if something more natural could be made or purchased. Here's a summary of my investigation:

I tried making my own jasmine syrup using flowers from the plant growing (and blooming) in my back yard. There are two problems with this: First, you must harvest an enormous number of flowers and second, jasmine fragrance is very hard to stabilize in an aqueous solution (water), and it quickly fades after infusion. I think the same would hold true if you wanted to make syrup using jasmine tea as a base.

I looked into buying an essential jasmine oil—the best of which are obscenely expensive because of how many flowers it takes to make it (e.g. 1,000 lbs of flowers yield approximately one pound of liquid)—but these oils are apparently not suitable for use as a food because of the oil used to make them.

I purchased a "natural" syrup from a place called Berry Farm. I found this to be very sweet (it contains fructose) but not particularly fragrant or complex. I should also note that Monin makes jasmine syrup, too, but I was unable to obtain it locally.

Recently I tried a new organic jasmine-flavored liqueur from Modern Spirits Group. It is part of their Fruit Lab line and is called Theia. It was clearly better than any of the other syrups I had tried and only mildly alcoholic (17%). I'd highly recommend trying Andrew's drink with it.

## KUMQUAT MARMALADE

*The General Lee, Matty Eggleston*

8 large kumquats

¾ cup sugar

¼ cup water

· Coarsely puree the kumquats using a small food processor.

· Combine the puree with the sugar and water in a saucepan.

· Bring to a low boil over a medium heat.

· Stir until the mixture becomes translucent and thickens.

· Remove the saucepan from the heat and allow the mixture to cool.

· Transfer to a jar or plastic container and store, covered, in the refrigerator.

*Notes:*

*This keeps almost indefinitely but over time the marmalade may become a little bitter because the seeds are pureed along with the fruit.*

*If the mixture seems too thin when heating it, you may add more pureed fruit to correct it. Similarly you can add more water to thin it if it seems overly thick.*

## LAVENDER SYRUP

*Kentucky Tuxedo, David Nelson*

1 cup of water

½ cup sugar

¼ oz. fresh lavender buds

· Wrap the lavender in a piece of cheesecloth and tie into a bundle.

· Heat the water and the sugar in a small saucepan.

· Stir the water to dissolve the sugar.

· When the water boils, add the lavender bundle.

· Remove from the heat immediately and cover tightly.

· Let stand for 15–20 minutes.

· Remove and discard the lavender.

· Allow the syrup to cool.

· Strain the syrup, transfer to a jar or plastic container and store, covered, in the refrigerator.

*Notes:*

*Makes enough for about 16 cocktails. It keeps for several months in the refrigerator.*

*The recipe calls for fresh lavender, not dried lavender, which is much stronger in flavor and scent. Dried lavender may be substituted by cutting the amount used by half or even two-thirds.*

## LAVENDER-INFUSED HONEY SYRUP

*Smallflower, Anu Apte*

1 cup water

¼ cup dried lavender

½ cup honey

· Bring the water to a boil and remove from the heat.

· Combine the lavender, honey, and hot water in a bowl.

· Stir to dissolve the honey.

· Allow the lavender to steep until the water is cool (about 30 minutes).

· Strain the mixture through a fine-mesh sieve to remove the lavender.

· Transfer to a jar or plastic container and store, covered, in the refrigerator.

*Notes:*

*Makes enough for about 16 cocktails. It keeps for about one month in the refrigerator.*

*See the note under "Lavender Syrup" about substituting dried lavender for fresh.*

# LIME–THAI PEPPER TINCTURE

*Reppiña, Andrew Friedman*

4 limes

½ bottle (375 ml) Everclear grain alcohol

10 dried red Thai chilies

3 oz. Simple Syrup (see note below)

¼ cup water

· Peel the limes using a wide blade peeler.

· Freeze the peels overnight.

· Place prepared peels in a 1-pint jar with a tight-fitting lid.

· Pour the Everclear into the jar and seal.

· Infuse the peels for 10–12 days, shaking once or twice a day.

· Filter the infusion through a coffee filter and return to the jar.

· Let stand for two days and then filter again.

· Carefully remove the seeds from the dry chilies.

· Add the seeded chilies to the infusion.

· Let stand for two more days.

· Filter the infusion again through a coffee filter.

· Add the simple syrup and water.

*Notes:*

*Makes enough for about 12 cocktails. It keeps almost indefinitely, though it may throw some sediment over time.*

*Andrew says freezing the peels helps to release their essential oils.*

*Ten days should be sufficient to infuse the lime peels if you are using the 180-proof Everclear. If you are using a lower-proof spirit, then you may need to extend the infusing time to 12 days or more. Whatever you use, the resulting infusion should be bright green and taste distinctly of limes.*

*If you cannot find dried red Thai chilies, you can use almost any other kind of dried chili as long as it's very hot. I used arbol chilies and chose not to remove the seeds.*

*A recipe for simple syrup is provided in this appendix.*

# LIME-WHEY MIXTURE

*Brace, Jennifer Colliau*

3 oz. lime juice

8 oz. nonfat milk

· Mix the lime juice and nonfat milk in a nonreactive bowl.

· Let it sit for a couple of minutes to curdle.

· Strain this mixture through a coarse-mesh sieve.

· Strain again several more times through progressively finer sieves and filters, ultimately straining through a dampened kitchen cloth to remove all the solids.

· At this point the mixture will be pale green and just slightly cloudy.

· Transfer to a jar or plastic container and store, covered, in the refrigerator.

*Notes:*

*Makes enough for about four cocktails.*

*Jennifer has written at length about this ingredient on her blog at http://smallhandbartender.blogspot.com/2009/04/whey.html*

## MAPLE SYRUP GASTRIQUE

*Still Life with Apples, After Cézanne, Daniel Hyatt*

2 oz. apple cider vinegar

4 oz. grade B maple syrup

1 small cinnamon stick

1 whole clove

1 black peppercorn

· Combine all the ingredients in a small saucepan and bring to a boil.

· Reduce the heat and simmer for 10 minutes.

· Remove from the heat and, using a slotted spoon, remove the spices.

· Allow the mixture to cool.

· Transfer to a jar or plastic container and store, covered, in the refrigerator.

*Notes:*

*Makes enough for about 10 cocktails. It keeps almost indefinitely in the refrigerator.*

## ORGEAT (AKA ORGEAT SYRUP)

*William Orange, Jimmy Patrick*

*Orgeat is a thick sweet syrup made using blanched raw almonds, and sometimes apricot kernels, in which the oils from the nuts have been extracted by soaking them in hot water for several hours, and to which sugar and small amounts of orange flower and/or rose water have been added. Originally made from barley in Italy, where it was called orzata, it was used as a substitute for milk in the days before refrigeration allowed milk to be transported very far from the farms where it was produced. In the Latin and South American countries, rice and other nuts are used in place of the almonds to create horchata (to which cinnamon, vanilla and sometimes milk has been added).*

*Today most commercial orgeat (almond) syrups are made using corn sweeteners and artificial flavoring. One exception is Monin, a brand that can be purchased in some places in the United States or through the web. If you are fortunate enough to live in the San Francisco bay area you can purchase excellent all-natural orgeat made by Jennifer Colliau's Small Hand Foods. (Note: Jennifer is one of the bartenders in this book.) Jennifer's syrups are available for sale at Cask in San Francisco, CA and Ledger's Liquors in Berkeley, CA.*

*Those who wish to make their own orgeat will find a wealth of recipes available to them on the Internet. Here are the links to two that I have used in the past:*

*http://scottesrum.com/2008/06/22/orgeat*

*http://underhill-lounge.flannestad. com/2008/07/12/orgeat-tales-version*

## PEAR FOAM

*Pear Sonata, Joel Baker*

7 oz. pear nectar

3 oz. St. Germain elderflower liqueur

2½ oz. egg whites

· Fill a 500-ml whipped cream canister with the pear nectar, elderflower liqueur, and egg whites.

· Seal the canister and shake to mix the ingredients.

· Charge with one nitrous oxide cartridge and shake.

· Refrigerate for one hour.

· Charge with another cartridge and shake again before using.

*Notes:*

*Makes enough for at least 10 cocktails.*

*The foam will keep for several days in the refrigerator.*

*Always remember to shake the canister immediately before using.*

## PECAN SYRUP

*Smoke Signals, Evan Zimmerman*

1 cup raw pecan halves

1 cup water

½ cup sugar

· Preheat the oven to 350 degrees F.

· Spread the pecans on a baking sheet.

· Toast the pecans until fragrant, about 10 minutes.

· Remove the pecans from the oven and allow them to cool.

· Bring the water and sugar to a boil in a medium saucepan.

· Add the roasted pecans and simmer over medium heat for 12 minutes.

· Remove from the heat and let cool.

· Strain twice, discarding the pecans when finished.

· Transfer to a jar or plastic container and store, covered, in the refrigerator.

*Notes:*

*Makes enough for about 10 cocktails. It will keep indefinitely in the refrigerator.*

## PRICKLY PEAR JUICE

*La Tuna Te Toca, H. Joseph Ehrmann*

12 red tunas (AKA prickly pears)

· Juice the tunas using a centrifugal juicer, such as a Champion.

· Put the juice in a squeeze bottle and store in the refrigerator.

· Shake well before each use.

*Notes:*

*It will keep fresh for several days if refrigerated.*

*Take care when handling the tunas as they have fine spines on them. You may wish to use rubber gloves.*

*The juice will become gelatinous over time but you can shake it and keep using it. Prickly pear juice freezes well too.*

*Both green and red tunas may be available, but for this recipe you want the red ones. The peak of the season for these fruits in California is September through November, although the season is somewhat longer in Mexico. Xoconochtlis, a related fruit that is found through the spring, is not an acceptable substitute.*

## ROASTED PINEAPPLE FEATHERS

*Reppiña, Andrew Friedman*

One half of a fresh pineapple, peeled and cored

· Preheat the oven to 250 degrees F and line a baking sheet with parchment paper or a silicone baking mat.

· Cut the pineapple lengthwise into two pieces.

· Using a very sharp chef's knife carefully cut the pineapple into 1/8" thick slices.

· Lay the resulting "feathers" on the prepared baking sheet.

· Bake until the "feathers" are almost dry and slightly browned on the edges, about 15– 30 minutes.

· Remove the pineapple from the oven and let cool.

· Store in a covered glass dish lined with a sheet of parchment.

*Notes:*

*The pineapple needs to be halved on the long axis (top to bottom) and not horizontally (across the core).*

*Andrew's original recipe specified using a mandoline to slice the pineapple but I found it was easier to just use a knife.*

*You may want to turn the "feathers" over as they roast in the oven so they dry evenly on both sides.*

## SAFFRON SHARBAT

*Saffron Sandalwood Sour, Anu Apte*

1¼ cups water

2 cups sugar

¼ cup rosewater

Saffron Extract (see next recipe)

· Mix the water and sugar in a heavy saucepan.

· Heat and stir until all the sugar is dissolved.

· In a small bowl, add the rosewater to the saffron extract. Then add this mixture to the sugar syrup.

· Simmer for five minutes.

· Remove from the heat and let cool.

· Transfer to a jar or plastic container and store, covered, in the refrigerator.

*Notes:*

*Makes enough for about 16 cocktails. It will keep indefinitely.*

*You may leave the saffron threads in the finished syrup or remove them.*

*This syrup can also be used to make soft drinks when mixed with some lime juice and soda water.*

## SAFFRON EXTRACT

1 tbsp. boiling water

Generous ¼ tsp. saffron threads

· Put 1 tbsp. boiling water into a small bowl (it's easiest to use a microwave to bring it to a boil).

· Crush the saffron threads between your thumb and finger and add to the hot water.

· Let it steep for 15 minutes.

## SAL DE GUSANO

*La Tuna Te Toca, H. Joseph Ehrmann*

This salt mixture is made with ground dried chilies and the worms that live in the agave plant, which have been toasted. These are the same worms added as a marketing gimmick to bottles of some mezcals (generally a sign of a bad mezcal). Since the agave plants (also called Maguey, pronounced "ma-GAY") are abundant in Oaxaca, these worms were one of the earliest forms of protein in the Oaxacan diet and part of the local cuisine. These worms actually have a unique flavor. Unless you're going to Oaxaca, look for this ingredient in your local Latin markets and you may just get lucky.

When making the cocktail, rim the glass with a little lime juice and then some sal de gusano.

*Notes:*

*This ingredient is extremely hard to locate. I tried many sources on the Internet: Nada. If you live in San Francisco, try La Oaxaquena located at 2128 Mission Street, though I was never successful finding it there. Or go to Elixir and pester H. to make one for you.*

## SIMPLE SYRUP (1:1) AND RICH SIMPLE SYRUP (2:1)

8 oz. water

8 oz. (or 16 oz. if making a rich syrup) white sugar

· Put the water and sugar in a saucepan.

· Bring the mixture to a boil, stirring frequently.

· Reduce heat to a low simmer and continue stirring until the sugar is dissolved and the syrup is clear.

· Remove from heat and allow the syrup to cool.

· Transfer to a jar or plastic container and store, covered, in the refrigerator.

*Notes:*

*It keeps almost indefinitely.*

*Unless stated otherwise, "simple syrup" means the 1:1 version.*

*Some bartenders will specify the use of organic unrefined sugar instead of white. Other than being organic, this product is pretty much as refined as regular white sugar. The resulting syrup will be slightly less clear and a little grayish in color.*

## SMOKED CIDER AIR

*Still Life with Apples, After Cézanne, Daniel Hyatt*

1 liter pasteurized (clear) apple cider

¼ tsp. liquid smoke concentrate

1½ grams soy lecithin granules

½ gram xanthan gum

· Pour the cider into an 8-quart white food-grade plastic container.

· Add the liquid smoke, soy lecithin, and xanthan gum.

· Using an immersion blender held just below the surface, mix and froth the mixture to form a thick layer of foam.

· Skim the very top of the foam—the driest part—which is the "air" that is added to the cocktail.

· Blend again as necessary to make more foam and "air."

*Notes:*

*Let me begin by saying that while making "Smoked Cider Air" requires some odd ingredients, special equipment, and unusual techniques, anyone who undertakes it will be rewarded by being able to savor a most excellent cocktail, one of my favorites in the book. And barring that, you can always visit Daniel Hyatt at Alembic in San Francisco and have him make one for you.*

*After some spectacular failed experiments in scaling this recipe down, I have concluded that it must be made using the quantities specified above if it is to come out right. It seems wasteful to make this much unless one is making a lot of drinks (since you can get an almost infinite amount of the "air" from a liter of cider by replenishing the lecithin and xanthan gum when it stops foaming). The various problems I encountered when trying to quarter the recipe (the difficulty measuring vanishingly small amounts of xanthan gum, inadequate foaming, and catastrophic precipitation of the lecithin when put on the drink), however, have led me to this conclusion.*

*It is also very important to do the blending in a container that is sufficiently deep and wide. The recommended 8-quart white food-grade container is very affordable and can be purchased at almost any restaurant supply store. I'd also get a lid to go with it.*

*Xanthan gum can be found at some specialty spice stores, Indian groceries, cake baking supply stores, and of course on the Internet. If you can't find xanthan gum, you may try tragacanth gum, which may be easier to find. You'll probably have to tinker with the amount, but keep in mind it's the lecithin that creates the "air"—the gum simply helps to stabilize it.*

*You will need a precision electronic scale accurate to less than a gram in order to measure the xanthan and the lecithin. You might ask around and see if you can borrow one.*

*Finally, unless (or even) when it is very dry, the "air" will have a tendency to precipitate some amount of lecithin into the cocktail once it has been spooned on top. (My conjecture is that this is a reaction with the acid in the Maple Syrup Gastrique, another home-made ingredient used in this cocktail.) In extreme cases, you will have a literal rain of lecithin pouring into the otherwise translucent cocktail. In this case, there's not much to do but "sink it" and start again.*

## SMOKED ICE

*Smoke Signals, Evan Zimmerman*

Distilled water

2 metal loaf or medium sized aluminum foil roasting pans

Hickory chips for smoking

· Prepare one pan by drilling or punching a number of small (⅛"– ¼") rather evenly spaced holes on the bottom.

· Fill the second pan with water and freeze overnight.

· Remove the pan from freezer and allow the ice to melt just enough to release the block from the pan.

· Place some hickory chips in a smoker and set to the lowest temperature possible.

· Transfer the ice block from the pan in which it was frozen into the perforated pan.

· Place the pan containing the ice in the smoker, with the other pan placed beneath it to collect the smoked water from the ice as it melts.

· Turn off the smoker after the ice has completely melted, and collect the pan with the smoked water in it.

· Place it back in the freezer and freeze completely.

· Once frozen, remove block from the pan.

· Carefully cut 2-by-2 inch blocks out of the ice with an ice pick or a serrated knife.

· Return to the freezer briefly to harden.

*Notes:*

*I used a couple of 13-by-10 inch aluminum foil roasting pans instead of the metal bread loaf pans specified in Evan's original recipe. It was also easy to punch slits in the bottom of these using the tip of a sharp knife.*

*If you are using a barbecue (or a smoker without wire shelves in it) you can place a small wire rack between the pans to stack them and then place these in the center of the grill.*

*This ice is very smoky. You probably don't want to let it come into contact with other ice in your freezer, and whatever container you used to make the ice block will probably be forever tainted with hickory smoke. In fact, I recommend re-freezing the smoked water in a new container instead of using the pan that came out of the smoker. I used a couple of plastic "to go" food containers (about 6" x 4" x 2").*

## TAHITIAN VANILLA–INFUSED ST. ELIZABETH ALLSPICE DRAM

*St. Astor, Christine D'Abrosca*

150 ml. St. Elizabeth Allspice Dram

¼ Tahitian vanilla bean, split lengthwise

· Place the vanilla bean into a 4-ounce jar with a tight-fitting lid.

· Pour the St. Elizabeth Allspice Dram over the bean and seal the jar.

· Let stand for about 24 hours, at which point you should be able to clearly taste the vanilla in the dram.

· Remove the vanilla bean, discard, and reseal the jar.

*Notes:*

*Makes enough for about 10 cocktails. It keeps indefinitely.*

*Using a Tahitian vanilla bean is crucial, as it is milder than beans from Madagascar or Mexico.*

*Personally, I would have thought the dram would overpower the vanilla, but it doesn't. I did two blind taste tests, and in both cases the testers could discern the difference between the plain and infused dram.*

## TEQUILA POR MI AMANTE

*El Globo Rojo, Jim Romdall*

2 pint baskets of fresh strawberries

16 oz. El Jimador reposado tequila

· Hull and quarter the strawberries and place into a 2-quart glass jar with a tight-fitting lid.

· Add the tequila to the jar.

· Infuse for three to four weeks, storing the jar in a cool place.

· Strain through a fine-mesh strainer, pressing firmly on the strawberries with the back of a large spoon to extract as much liquid as possible.

*Notes:*

*Makes enough for about 10 cocktails. Although it seems like this should last almost indefinitely (since it is alcohol-based), it should be used within a couple of weeks, since it will oxidize.*

*This is based on a recipe from Charles Baker's The Gentleman's Companion (1934).*

## THAI CHILI TINCTURE

*Carter Beats the Devil, Erik Adkins*

*Dragon Variation, Jon Santer*

Thai chilies (see note below)

Wray & Nephew overproof rum

· Completely fill a small jar with the chilies from which you have removed the stems.

· Cover with the rum and let sit for two weeks.

· Strain out the chilies.

· Carefully transfer the tincture to a dropper bottle.

· Mark clearly to avoid accidents.

*Notes:*

*The tincture will keep indefinitely.*

*The number of chilies required for this recipe will depend on the size of the jar you are using to make the tincture.*

*Take real care when handling the chilies as well as the resulting tincture, which will be very hot. You may want to wear rubber gloves when removing the stems from the chilies and putting them in the jar.*

## LOS ANGELES

## BARS

There are many, many, wonderful bars in the cities represented in this book. Too many for us to list completely. So here is a list of the establishments featured in our book.

And please read this important note about the migratory patterns of bartenders:

Bartenders tend to move around from job to job a lot. While we made every effort to update this book right up to the date of its printing, inevitably our featured bartenders will have moved on in some cases. However, every bar listed below is of highest quality, and you are sure to have an excellent experience even if the bartender you fell in love with from reading this book is no longer there. In all likelihood, you will find another fine bartender there, who will show you a good time, and let you know where to find the person whom you came to see. At that point, the bar crawl is officially on! Follow us, we will never steer you wrong, people.

**Copa d'Oro**
217 Broadway, Santa Monica, CA 90401
310.576.3030 (copadoro.com)

**The Edison**
108 W. 2nd St #101, Los Angeles, CA 90012
213.613.0000 (edisondowntown.com)

**The Hungry Cat**
1535 N. Vine St, Los Angeles, CA 90028
323.462.2155 (thehungrycat.com)

**Malo**
4326 W. Sunset Blvd, Los Angeles, CA 90029
323.664.1011 (malorestaurant.com)

**Osteria Mozza**
6602 Melrose Ave, Los Angeles, CA 90038
323.297.0100 (mozza-la.com)

**The Roger Room**
370 N. La Cienega Blvd, Los Angeles, CA 90048
310.854.1300

**Seven Grand**
515 W. 7th St, Los Angeles, CA, 90014
213.614.0737 (sevengrand.la)

**The Varnish**
118 E. 6th St, Los Angeles, CA 90014
213.622.9999 (thevarnishbar.com)

**Alembic**
1725 Haight St, San Francisco, CA 94117
415.666.0822 (alembicbar.com)

**Bar Agricole**
355 11th St, San Francisco, CA 94103
no phone as of this printing (baragricole.com)

**Beretta**
1199 Valencia St, San Francisco, CA 94110
415.695.1199 (berettasf.com)

**Bourbon & Branch**
501 Jones St, San Francisco, CA 94102
(bourbonandbranch.com)

**Cantina**
580 Sutter St, San Francisco, CA 94102
415.398.0195 (cantinasf.com)

**Clock Bar**
The Westin St. Francis
335 Powell St, San Francisco, CA 94102
415.397.9222 (michaelmina.net/clockbar.com)

**Delarosa**
2175 Chestnut St, San Francisco, CA 94123
415.673.7100 (delarosasf.com)

**Elixir**
3200 16th St, San Francisco, CA 94103
415.552.1633 (elixirsf.com)

**Flora**
1900 Telegraph Ave, Oakland, CA 94612
510.286.0100 (floraoakland.com)

**Heaven's Dog**
1148 Mission St, San Francisco, CA 94103
415.863.6008 (heavensdog.com)

**Lion & Compass**
1023 N. Fair Oaks Ave, Sunnyvale, CA 94089
408.745.1260 (lionandcompass.com)

**Nopa**
560 Divisadero St, San Francisco, CA 94117
415.864.8643 (nopasf.com)

**Range**
842 Valencia St, San Francisco, CA 94110
415.282.8283 (rangesf.com)

**The Slanted Door**
1 Ferry Building #3, San Francisco, CA 94111
415.861.8032 (slanteddoor.com)

**Smuggler's Cove**
650 Gough St, San Francisco, CA 94102
415.869.1900 (smugglerscovesf.com)

**Starbelly**
3583 16th St, San Francisco, CA 94114
415.252.7500 (starbellysf.com)

**50 Plates**
333 NW 13th Ave, Portland, OR 97209
503.228.5050 (50plates.com)

**Aqua**
151 NW Monroe Ave, Corvallis, OR 97330
541.752.0262 (aquacorvallis.com)

**Beaker & Flask**
720 SE Sandy Blvd, Portland, OR 97214
503.235.8180 (beakerandflask.com)

**Branch**
2926 NE Alberta St, Portland, OR 97211
503.206.6266 (branchwhiskeybar.com)

**Clyde Common**
1014 SW Stark St, Portland, OR 97205
503.228.3333 (clydecommon.com)

**Downward Dog/Cloud 9**
130 SW 1st St, Corvallis, OR 97333
541.753.9900 (drinkthedog.com)

**Laurelhurst Market**
3155 E. Burnside, Portland, OR, 97214
503.206.3097 (laurelhurstmarket.com)

**Teardrop Lounge**
1015 NW Everett St, Portland, OR, 97209
503.445.8109 (teardroplounge.com)

**ten01**
1001 NW Couch St, Portland, OR, 97209
503.226.3463 (ten-01.com)

**Barrio**
1420 12th Ave, Seattle, WA 98122
206.588.8105 (barriorestaurant.com)

**Liberty**
517 15th Ave E, Seattle, WA 98112
206.323.9898 (libertybars.com)

**Mistral Kitchen**
2020 Westlake Avenue, Seattle, WA 98121
209.623.1922 (mistral-kitchen.com)

**Moshi Moshi**
5324 Ballard Ave, Seattle, WA 98107
206.971.7424 (moshiseattle.com)

**Naga** (at Chantanee Thai Restaurant)
601 108th Ave NE Ste 100, Bellevue WA 98004
425.455.3226 (chantanee.com)

**Oliver's Twist**
6822 Greenwood Ave N, Seattle, WA 98103
206.706.6673 (oliverstwistseattle.com)

**Rob Roy**
2332 2nd Ave, Seattle, WA 98121
206.956.8423 (robroyseattle.com)

**Sambar**
425 NW Market St, Seattle, WA 98107
206.781.4883 (sambarseattle.com)

**Spur**
113 Blanchard St, Seattle, WA 98121
206.728.6706 (spurseattle.com)

Left Coast Libations

**Tavern Law**
1406 12th Ave, Seattle, WA 98122
206.322.9734 (tavernlaw.com)

**Union**
1400 1st Ave, Seattle, WA 98101
206.838.8000 (unionseattle.com)

**Vessel**
1312 5th Ave, Seattle, WA 98101
206.652.0521 (vesselseattle.com)

**Zig Zag Café**
1501 Western Ave, Seattle, WA 98101
206.625.1146 (zigzagcafe.net)

**Chambar Gastown**
562 Beatty St, Vancouver, BC V6B
604.879.7119 (chambar.com)

**The Diamond Gastown**
6 Powell St, Vancouver, BC V6A
604.408.2891 (di6mond.com)

**West**
2881 Granville St, Vancouver, BC V6H
604.738.8938 (westrestaurant.com)

## BARTENDER BLOGS

Where are they now, what are they thinking, when do they get out of the slammer?

**Andrew Bohrer**
caskstrength.wordpress.com

**Jamie Boudreau**
spiritsandcocktails.wordpress.com

**Jennifer Colliau**
smallhandbartender.blogspot.com

**H. Joseph Ehrmann**
elixirsf.blogspot.com

**Daniel Hyatt**
alembicbar.blogspot.com

**Lance Mayhew**
mylifeontherocks.com

**Jeffrey Morgenthaler**
www.jeffreymorgenthaler.com

**Jimmy Patrick**
www.mixographer.com

**David Shenaut**
onthehouse.com

**Keith Waldbauer**
movingatthespeedoflife.blogspot.com

**Neyah White**
ohgroup.blogspot.com

## OTHER REALLY GOOD STUFF

**Cask**
*caskspirits.com, 17 3rd St, San Francisco, 94102, 415.424.4844*

From the owners of Bourbon & Branch, a lovely liquor store offering "exceptional spirits, small production California wines, and boutique hand-crafted beers." They have some pretty sweet bar tools, too. Kevin Diedrich was manager here until he abandoned us.

**John Walker and Company**
*johnwalker.com, 175 Sutter St, San Fancisco, 94104, 800.350.5577*

A seminal and well stocked liquor store in business since 1933, specializing in highest quality and hard to find spirits and wines. Dominic Venegas acts as their spirits buyer.

**San Francisco Cocktail Week**
*sfcocktailweek.com*

"A Week In Honor of San Francisco's Vibrant Cocktail Culture" held each May. A wide variety of cocktail events held at several restaurants, bars, and event spaces around the city. Throw a rock at an SF Cocktail Week event and it will hit an LCL contributor, so for God's sake don't throw a rock at an SF Cocktail Week event!

**The Beverage Academy**
*beverageacademy.com*

San Francisco-based school offering classes in all the major spirits, Tiki, Cocktails 101, and Barbary Coast Cocktails. Classes taught at Bourbon & Branch. Instructors include Jon Santer, Dominic Venegas, Kevin Diedrich, and Ryan Fitzgerald.

## Beverage Alcohol Resource

*beveragealcoholresource.com*

"The spirits and mixology equivalent of a Masters of Wine or Master Sommelier program." Located in New York City and featuring instructors David Wondrich, Dale DeGroff, Steve Olson, Paul Pacult, Andy Seymour, and Doug Frost. At least nine LCL contributors are graduates, and many more will be soon.

## United States Bartenders' Guild

*usbg.org*

National guild with chapters in several cities, including Los Angeles and San Francisco. Offers a Masters Accreditation program for bartenders. The majority of LCL contributors from Los Angeles and San Francisco hold positions of leadership in their respective chapters.

## Oregon Bartenders Guild

*oregonbarguild.org*

"The Oregon Bartenders Guild was formed in 2007 to help bring together like-minded bar professionals and amateur mixologists, and to help raise awareness of Oregon bartending within the state and around the world." LCL contributors Jeffrey Morgenthaler, David Shenaut, and Chris Churilla are board members. James Pierce, Daniel Shoemaker, and Kinn Edwards are members.

## Washington State Bartenders Guild

*wsbg.org*

State-wide independent guild formed in 2008 comprised of "professionals and enthusiasts with an enduring mission to elevate the standard of bartending as a craft." Andrew Friedman is president, Keith Waldbauer vice president, and Andrew Bohrer secretary. Every other Seattle bartender in this book is a member, except for that Jay Kuehner guy. What's his deal anyway?

## Le Mixeur

*lemixeur.blogspot.com*
Ted Munat's blog. A source of continued mirth and merriment for all.

## Stirred, Not Shaken

*Stirrednotshakenblog.wordpress.com*
Michael Lazar's blog. Focused on homemade ingredients and original cocktail recipes.

## The Cocktail Chronicles

*www.cocktailchronicles.com*
Paul Clarke's blog. Excellent articles on cocktails and cocktail culture.

# INDEX OF SPIRITS

## S

## T

## V

## W

# EPILOGUE

We knew going into this project that bartenders were scurrilous little creatures, and we tried to warn you, dear reader. Remember all that hoity-toity mumbo jumbo in the foreword about the cocktail world being a "fluid process that changes and grows by the moment"? Well that concept spreads to the careers of bartenders. We'll never print a book that's entirely up-to-date. For that, please refer to the Left Coast Libations web site and the Left Coast Libations blog, where we will make ongoing and diligent efforts to update the masses on the movements of our favorite bartenders. (Incidentally, rumors that we implanted GPS tracking devices just beneath the skin on the back of the neck of each bartender are scandalous...and only partially true.)

In one last desperate attempt to make this book seem timely and relevant, here's a wee little epilogue...

- Joseph Brooke left Copa d'Oro and became Diretor of Spirits for The Edison. The reason for the move? Probably acting and a girl again.

- Jon Santer left Martin Miller's and became Ambassdor for Hendrick's Gin. His new gig keeps him busy and makes bartending shifts sporadic, but he's certain to turn up at some of the finest places from time to time.

- Kevin Diedrich returned to the Left Coast, and like a mother being reunited with her runaway child, we alternated joyous weeping with slapping him silly. Possible spots to find him in the future include Rye, Bar Agricole, Smuggler's Cove, Clock Bar...you know the drill by now.

- H. Joseph Ehrmann and Marco Dionysos, along with LCL Hero Scott Beattie, launched the "Experiential Cocktail Catering Service," H.M.S. Cocktails. They'll be using their considerable skills to take liquid catering to a whole new level. (HMSCocktails.com)

☞ Jackie Patterson started at Smuggler's Cove, then left Smugler's Cove (but stayed at Heaven's Dog) to consult and design the bar program at a new spot opening in Berkeley, and also to collaborate with...

☞ Jennifer Colliau, the mastermind behind Small Hand Foods. Jackie and Jennifer will be working together to create their own line of liqueurs. Oh boy!

☞ Lance Mayhew became resident whiskey writer for About.com and forgot other spirits existed, until he became a representative for Oxley Gin.

☞ Kinn Edwards realized the dream and opened his own bar and restaurant (along with friend and chef Adam Kekahuna). The place will be called Loca Luna. Theme will be Latin fusion, or as we lushes like to call it, "Rum and Tequila!" (localunacorvallis.com)

☞ David Nelson continued to work with chef/owners Brian McCracken and Dana Tough as bar manager at Tavern Law, but ceded those duties at Spur. Or so he claims. I bet he sneaks over there from time to time.

☞ Tara McLaughlin became bar manager at Grey Gallery and Bar, where she attempts to perform a similar resuscitation to what she once did at Rob Roy.

☞ Anu Apte became a Master Shaolin Fighter/Dancer and was never heard from again...

# ABOUT THE AUTHORS

## Ted Munat

Ted Munat is a freelance cocktail writer based in Seattle, Washington. Under the moniker Le Mixeur, he has created a most irreverent blog (lemixeur.blogspot.com) and orchestrated a number of cocktail events promoting bartenders, craft cocktails, and a new cocktail community. Ted shares a mission with his loose federation of Munat Brothers to never pay for a drink again. This book is another surreptitious step in this devious plan.

## Michael Lazar

100 cocktails and over 40 homemade ingredients: they had to be made, tasted, and tested, some several times. Michael Lazar, the mad kitchen scientist cum bartender for Left Coast Libations, did it all. Distillate of his experience can be found throughout this book in the form of notes and scribblings intended to enlighten both neophyte and professional. Further excerpts from his secret diaries can be found on his blog "Stirred, Not Shaken" along with his own original cocktail recipes and frequent musings on exotic citrus and semi-toxic cordials. No longer satisfied to simply test and write about cocktails, Michael now makes and serves them regularly to willing guests at venues (underground or otherwise) throughout the San Francisco Bay Area.

## Jenn Farrington

Jenn Farrington is an advertising, editorial and documentary photographer who shoots travel, lifestyle, food and beverage. Select publications include: Gourmet, Wine and Spirits, USA Today, San Francisco Chronicle and C Magazine. She shot the location photos for the book *Tequila: A Guide to Types, Flights, Cocktails and Bites* by Joanne Weir / Ten Speed Press. International photo travels include: Egypt, Israel, St. Martin, UK, Canada, Mexico, Netherlands, Thailand, and Czech Republic. Jenn's current travel schedule and new work can be seen at jennfarrington.com.